GETTING YOUR MONEY'S WORTH FROM HOME CONTRACTORS

GETTING YOUR MONEY'S WORTH FROM HOME CONTRACTORS

by MIKE McCLINTOCK

Harmony Books / New York

For Triny

   Published by Harmony Books, a division of Crown Publishers, Inc., One Park Avenue, New York, New York 10016 and published simultaneously in Canada by General Publishing Company Limited.
HARMONY BOOKS and colophon are trademarks of Crown Publishers, Inc.
   Manufactured in the United States of America

Library of Congress Cataloging in Publication Data

McClintock, Michael, 1945–
   Getting your money's worth from home contractors.

   1.Dwellings—Maintenance and repair—Handbooks, manuals, etc. I. Title.
TH4817.M37   643.7   82-883
                                  AACR2

ISBN: 0-517-543532 (hardcover)
          0-517-543540 (paper)

10 9 8 7 6 5 4 3 2 1
First Edition

Contents

Appendix:
CONSUMER INFORMATION SOURCES

How to Use This Book

No matter where you live or how handy you are, at some point you will have to rely on professional help to maintain, repair, and improve your home. It's just not possible to do every job yourself, even if you had the time and the inclination.

You may need a roofer, an exterminator, a locksmith, or an electrician, and when the time comes, you'll have a lot of questions. You'll get practical answers to questions like these in *Getting Your Money's Worth from Home Contractors*: How can I find reliable contractors? How can I evaluate their qualifications and their estimates for the job? How can I make a fair contract with them that protects my interests? What services do I have a right to expect, and what professional practices are standard? How can I evaluate their work, and what can I do if problems develop over time or money or quality?

Picture yourself knowing the answers to these questions, eliminating the fly-by-nighters and the ripoffs, all *before* the job begins. You can do it because *Getting Your Money's Worth from Home Contractors* has a completely new approach for consumers: it covers the people who do the work, not the endless, technical details of the work itself.

I've done repair work and renovations, built new homes, published more than 200 articles on home repair and improvement, talked to home consumers on the job and every week on a radio call-in show, and I can tell you this: you don't have to know all the details of a job to hire a contractor who can do that job well. You don't have to know all about ground fault circuit interrupters to get quality results from an electrician, or all about counterflashing to get your money's worth from a roofer. Let the professionals figure out the nitty-gritty details and solve the problems—that's their job. *Your* job is to hire the right contractor and now you'll be able to with the information in *Getting Your Money's Worth from Home Contractors*. Each home contractor is listed alphabetically and each entry is organized the same way. Here's what you'll find:

1. The range of services provided by the professional

2. The qualifications required to perform these services competently

3. The standards of professional practice you have a right to expect, either by custom or law

4. Telltale indicators that let you evaluate the quality of the professional's work

5. How to act on grievances over money, time, or quality if problems develop.

This information is very specific, and for good reason. As home consumers, all of us have been disappointed by a how-to article, a set of assembly instructions, or an owner's manual that appears complete but, in fact, leaves out crucial details. Incomplete information makes you vulnerable, and what's worse, the contractor knows you're vulnerable. The result of this mismatch? You may be in for substandard work at ripoff prices.

This book tips the odds back in your favor. Each entry includes the information you need, all the pertinent details: sources for recommendations, trade and professional associations, industry and government standards, procedures to verify a contractor's diagnosis and estimate, addresses, phone numbers, sources of additional technical and consumer information, and more.

In addition to the detailed entries, this book starts with the Consumer's Primer. It contains the most fundamental guidelines for five important operations that apply to every contractor: (1) shopping for professional services; (2) soliciting and evaluating estimates; (3) checking professional qualifications and recognizing substandard practices; (4) evaluating informal agreements and formal contracts; and (5) mediating grievances to achieve practical solutions.

There's more. *Getting Your Money's Worth from Home Contractors* also provides an extensive listing called Consumer Information Sources. It includes the names, addresses, and phone numbers (including many toll-free lines) of the regional offices of key federal agencies like the Department of Housing and Urban Development. Following this is a listing of consumer agencies by state, county, and city, across the country, and a list of all the toll-free telephone numbers for federal information centers, available in 85 cities in 37 states. These centers are staffed by people who have one job—to help you get the consumer information you need; if they don't have it, they can direct you to the consumer agency (whether federal, state, or local) that does.

I have mentioned the Better Business Bureau in many of the contractor entries. You can write The Council of Better Business Bureaus (1150 17 St. NW, Washington, DC 20036) for the current list of local bureaus or check in your local phone book. You may not need all the information in the Consumer Information Sources, but if you do, you'll be able to use it to get real results.

Quality products and services are available. There are many sources of consumer information on products, and you probably take the time and trouble to investigate products carefully before you buy. Now you'll be able to look at the other side of the coin—the people and the services behind the products, materials, and technology that make up your home environment. Now you'll be able to get the job done right the first time around, no matter how much experience you have with the care and feeding of your home. You'll be able to get quality work at a fair price.

Coping with Your Home

The Tillotsons bought their first house in October. In May, when water poured down the hill soaking every basement in the development, the Tillotsons discovered that the builder's corporation no longer existed. Two basement waterproofers gave the Tillotsons estimates of $2,500 to dig trenches around the house and add waterproofing membranes and drains. The Tillotsons took the third estimate, for pressure-pumping clay into the ground around the house, because it was cheaper ($1,400) and it wouldn't destroy their new shrubs and ground cover. The waterproofer said he was a factory-authorized dealer of the Clay Seal Co., and the local consumer protection agency had no complaints registered against him.

Two months later the basement flooded again. The Tillotsons lost a second, new wall-to-wall carpet and pad; their insurance agent couldn't find a company to pick up their homeowner's policy. The local building inspector told them clay-injection was worthless, and they discovered that the waterproofer had had no complaints lodged against him because he had been operating in the county only three months and it takes three months to process and record complaints. The Clay Seal Co. answered their complaint letter, saying that they sold rock and sand products to local contractors, were not a factory, and had no dealers. The Tillotsons finally got a loan and paid $3,000 (the price nearly a year later) to the right contractor to do the right job—a job their builder should have done before they moved in.

What's the answer when a disaster like this happens? Should you avoid potential problems and ripoffs by doing everything yourself? Think of all the work that goes into building, improving, repairing, and maintaining twentieth-century homes—everything from the jobs done by carpenters and general contractors to the efforts of painters and paperhangers. Can you imagine anyone having enough training and skill to do all this on his own?

Two hundred years ago self-sufficiency was a way of life. When you wanted shelter, you built it. When you needed food, you grew it or caught it. The early American homestead was self-sufficiency in its most complete form.

Today, you can't exercise squatter's rights in Scarsdale or Marin County. Try planting an acre of corn in the middle of Columbus Circle or Columbus, Ohio. There are limits to the do-it-yourself mania. After you've fixed your furnace, waterproofed your foundation, tarred the roof, installed the airtight stove, and (*pant, pant*) learned how to can, split wood, and hang wallpaper, when will you have time for your regular job?

Even if you try to get back to a simple way of life, even if you strip your home of the electronic, gadget-happy frills, there's just too much twentieth-century technology left to tackle on your own. Doing things yourself may be the modern equivalent of self-sufficiency homesteading, but at some point everyone has to rely on some professional help.

Sometimes the requirements and restrictions of professional licensing, building codes, public law, and technology-loaded equipment eliminate the possibility of doing it yourself. You can't be your own licensed electrician if you don't have a license. Many apartment dwellers and homeowners don't have the time, the credentials, or the inclination to refinish floors, install solar heating equipment, convert furnaces from oil to gas, or build their own swimming pools.

The alternative of using someone else's goods and services instead of doing and providing everything yourself started with the simple, efficient process of bartering. A barefoot farmer gave part of his crop to a hungry shoemaker. It made sense; there were no middle men. And one-on-one this system still works so well that the government has called bartering goods and services the "underground economy" because it flows below the federal tax structure.

Today many complex home products and services have to be provided by professionals. It's tough to build an efficient furnace or a foundation that won't crack and leak. But when you pay for complicated products and services you don't fully understand, it's even tougher to judge quality, to know if you're getting your money's worth. You can get a lot of help evaluating home products—many are inspected, rated, categorized, guaranteed, and warrantied at great length. They are analyzed by government agencies, industry trade associations, and consumer magazines. But what about the home services?

Many people buy a washing machine based on the rating in *Consumer Reports* magazine. But what about the dealer who sells the machine, the installer who hooks it up, and the repairman who fixes it? Every stick of lumber in a new home is grade-stamped, new air conditioners carry an energy-efficiency rating, but carpenters or refrigeration mechanics do not. That's the way it works now—the eggs are graded but not the chickens that lay them.

If you had to hire a locksmith or a tree surgeon every week of the year, you would certainly get good at it. After you had been through ten insulation contractors you'd be able to judge their professional standards, services, fees, and warranties accurately. But what a way to learn. Trial and error may be memorable, but it's usually painful and expensive as well.

Home services vary from contractor to contractor. There is no simple or statistical yardstick for talent, professionalism, or attention to detail. But there are concrete ways to evaluate the quality of a contractor and that is what this book is all about.

Why are we so keen to examine home products and so lax on home services? Products, of course, are finite, and easier to evaluate than services. The big problem here is our consumer conditioning. We have been swept along by the spirit of technology, the miracle of the microprocessor, the space-age kitchen. We have been led with slickly packaged products and incessant advertising to the conclusion that science solves problems, not scientists; that building materials make houses, not carpenters; that high-level technology creates quality, not high-level craftsmanship. It's an easy line to swallow because sometimes it's true. A home built with dense, heartwood beams and fire-code wallboard is more fire-resistant than a typical house. But if the electrician undersizes wiring, if the mason leaves open seams in the fireplace flue liner, even the highest-quality building materials can go up in smoke.

Have we misread the relative importance of products and services? How many times have you heard of an accident's being attributed not to mechanical breakdown but to human failing, to pilot error, or a nuclear technician's disregard of a pressure-gauge reading? The more you use materials and technology you don't understand, the more vulnerable you are. The more removed you become from the workings of your environment, the more you are at its mercy and have to depend on professionals to create and maintain that environment for you. Here are the possibilities. Faced with an increasingly complicated environment you can drop out and head for the wilderness. Conversely, you can earn, earn, earn and spend, spend, spend until your fingers develop calluses from punching all the buttons of gadget-happy electronic living. But there is a more reasonable middle ground. Apply that homesteading, do-it-yourself spirit where it is most effective, on things you understand. That leaves a lot of jobs requiring professional care and feeding. You can deal effectively with these jobs simply by concentrating on the services instead of the products, by examining the professionals instead of the equipment.

You don't need to know all the details it took the home contractors years to learn just as you don't have to run your own stress test on the ailerons of a plane before you buy a ticket. You don't need to know the mathematical formulas used to calculate home heating and cooling loads. But you should know how heating and cooling contractors operate, the language they use, the contracts they offer, and more. If you know the qualities and characteristics of a quality chicken, you don't have to know the biological mechanics of the egg.

When the time comes to hire a builder, an exterminator, or an electrician, when you bang into technology and systems beyond your experience, you will be dependent on their thoroughness, their honesty, their professionalism. No set of consumer guidelines can remove all the unknown elements of your exchanges with home contractors. But with a modest amount of crucial information about standards of professional practice, qualifications, and indicators of expertise, you can be much more than a passive, check-signing participant in the exchange.

You can't talk to a piece of technology—you can talk to a technician. You can ask him questions that go to the heart of the matter without dissecting every vein and artery. You can judge home contractors by comprehensible standards without deliberating over the technicalities of their trade.

With this approach you won't have to be completely self-sufficient. You won't have to be a full-time do-it-yourselfer. It's not an effortless, self-help magic wand that can solve all your problems, but it will get you your money's worth.

PART I:

THE CONSUMER'S PRIMER

The Primer provides a foundation, a starting point, for all the entries on home contractors that follow. It assumes you have had very little experience with contractors and suggests guidelines for five important operations that may be completely new to you. Following these guidelines are seven principles that you should try to abide by as a home consumer. For example, *trust your instincts,* trust your first impressions of a home contractor and hire him if everything else about him checks out. These principles will help you to have a greater success with home improvements and repairs.

Remember, the Primer contains fundamentals: it is only one part of *Getting Your Money's Worth.* Use it with the specific professional entries and the extensive appendix of "Consumer Information Sources" if you want to really get your money's worth.

Shopping for Professional Services

Are you an impulse buyer? Be honest now, do you empty the racks at supermarket checkout counters while you're waiting in line? You might buy a pack of gum on impulse, but how about a new car? You might sign up for a magazine subscription on a whim, but how about signing a home-improvement contract? No way, right? When a lot of money, time, and the disruption or safety of your household are involved, you've got to be careful. Better yet, you must be selective.

Selective is the key word: you've got to select the right professional for the job from several candidates. When your doctor advises you to have an operation, you usually get a second opinion. With home contractors, you must go a step further: always get at least three opinions; always talk to three or more contractors before making a commitment to any one. It's essential to see how the different contractors assess the job and what they are willing to offer.

But suppose your friendly next-door neighbor has a brother-in-law who's just the "best damn basement waterproofer in the county"? He may be the best and you may wind up protecting your home through him, but don't make the mistake of talking *only* to him, of giving him the exclusive right to your business. Resist the impulse to "move directly to go." The end result of hiring the neighbor's brother-in-law may be positive, but you'll miss the eye-opening experience of traveling around the board, of getting acquainted with the rules of the game, and taking a look at other prices and options.

Now, how do you get that list of three or more candidates? You can start with your best friend, your neighbor, or any other firsthand sources you can think of. Remember, that's firsthand sources—people you know, not know of.

This is usually the best source of recommendations. Why? Because friends and acquaintances have no ax to grind and nothing to gain from a recommendation. They're not likely to suggest a problem contractor. Also, you'll have firsthand access to the contractor's work. If your friend suggests a landscaper, you can see how his lawn looks and how well it has held up. If a contractor repaired the furnace, you can find out if he responded to a callback. Personal recommendations allow you to see the quality of the contractor's work firsthand.

The next-best source? Disinterested professional recommendations. For example, you can ask a local architect for the name of a reliable building contractor, or check with the banker who arranged your mortgage for the name of an experienced insulation contractor. Here you are requesting a professional's view of another professional's service, a building inspector's idea of a good electrician.

Disinterestedness is important; the recommendation is valuable *only* if the professional who made it does not stand to gain from the recommendation. If you're looking for an arborist or a landscaper, try the county agricultural agent. He will have some expertise in the field and probably knows most of the reliable, well-established firms. He has nothing to gain by recommending them.

This type of recommendation loses value, however, when the sponsor has something to gain if you pick his candidate for the job. For example, a nursery or garden-supply company will know several local landscapers, but they may sponsor the professional who buys supplies from them, whether he's the best one for the job or not. A building-supply dealer will have a natural tendency to give you the name of a general contractor who will, in turn, give him orders for lumber and shingles. Exercise your common sense to recognize and evaluate these potential conflicts of interest.

I make a distinction between recommendations and referrals. Recommendations can be positive or negative; they express a point of view, an opinion. Referrals are just names without positive or negative opinions attached to them. Referrals come out of the phone book or from a classified ad. They're neutral; just a name and number.

Some referrals can carry a reliable measuring stick of expertise. For example, if you are looking for a contractor to redo the kitchen in your new coop, you can get names out of the phone book, but it's better to call the National Home Improvement Council.

Naturally, trade associations and professional societies won't recommend one of their members over another, but they will provide the names of members near you who meet their minimal professional standards. These standards vary from field to field. For some professionals, like electricians and arborists, affiliation signals extensive education and a license to practice. For others, like basement waterproofers and siding specialists, affiliation may indicate only minimal field experience. Anyone can print up some business cards and call himself a house painter.

Affiliation with a professional society, however, is a positive indicator. Would a fly-by-nighter bother with the time, trouble, and money to join an association? Would he submit references or subscribe to a code of ethics? Probably not. But connection with an association is not a guarantee of quality work. It's not as good as a firsthand recommendation, but it is a way to increase the number of candidates for your job.

Soliciting and Evaluating Estimates

When you have a list of three or more candidates, then what? Talk to them—face to face. But first, you must have a clear idea of what the job is. This sounds obvious, but many people don't think out what they want done. They want a deck built, and maybe it should be redwood or pressure-treated timber, or wrap around the kitchen patio, or maybe not. If you don't have a firm grasp on what you require, all the contractors you talk to will come up with different suggestions and estimates.

This variety is wonderful, but you'll be comparing estimates the way you compare apples and oranges—with great difficulty. Whenever possible, come to grips with the purpose of the job, with its physical and financial limits, and the results you're looking for *before* calling in a professional. This doesn't mean you have to make a lot of technical decisions. Let the professionals do that. It does mean making your priorities clear, however. For example, the durability and maintenance-free characteristics of the deck may be paramount, whereas stretching its size may be secondary.

Sometimes apples and oranges are inevitable. It's a real problem, and there is not always a good solution. For example, say you notice that vegetables are growing old in your refrigerator before their time. You read the owner's manual and fiddle with the thermostat with no result. Then you call in three appliance servicemen. One says the compressor is shot, quotes a repair price of $400, and advises you to get a new refrigerator. Another serviceman says the thermostat is broken and quotes a $125 repair price. A third says the problem is simple: a low Freon level, probably from a very small, long-term leak. Recharging the system (putting in more of the refrigerant to bring the cooling system up to proper pressure) will cost about $45, including the service call. What do you do?

Here are some steps to help unravel the mystery. First: ask each contractor to explain the diagnosis in layman's terms (why did the compressor cut out; if it's shot, why is the refrigerator still cool even if it's not cold enough?). Second: ask each contractor why the diagnosis of his competitor is wrong. This is a good one. Sure it's a little testy; it may ruffle some feathers, but that's all right. A good diagnosis should be justifiable. Third: ask each contractor, hypothetically, if you accept his diagnosis and follow his advice, what guarantees can he make about the results. You need a working refrigerator; buying a new one is easy but may be an extreme solution. The $125 solution could be worthwhile but only if it lasts. The $45 solution is not much of a gamble at all. When you have gathered all this information, check the contractor's solution with an outside source. Look in the phone book for a factory-authorized repairman or a local store that handles your brand of refrigerator. Tell them the model, how old the appliance is, what the symptoms are, and ask what they think of the diagnosis.

There's more to an estimate than cost alone. Sure it's important, but pay close attention to guarantees of performance and factor in the source of the estimate. Is it from a first hand recommendation or a neutral, third-party referral?

There are a few things you should not do. At this point, don't tell the contractors how much you have to spend. If you do, count on an estimate that matches or exceeds this figure. Don't make any commitments. You can say that you're thinking seriously about adding a deck or replacing the refrigerator, but you want information right now, not a contract.

By the way, if you have already decided which contractor to use, it doesn't make much sense to ask others for estimates. When I built houses, I developed a sixth sense about requests for estimates that had no substance, that were only for comparison. And, like most builders, I didn't work too hard to get the fat out of my estimates for those jobs.

Finally, don't stifle the expertise and creativity of a professional by insisting on only apples. Don't say that the deck *must* be redwood, that it *must* be made of 2 x 6s, that it *must* be 3 feet off the ground. Ask for an estimate on your set of specifications, and tell the contractor to list separately any alternatives he thinks are better, with a separate price.

Remember: ask questions. Ask the builder to explain all the options—what the different materials cost, what services he provides, and more. Proceed with your eyes and ears open. Gather information, but don't shake any hands or sign any papers yet.

Checking on Minimal Professional Qualifications

This process should push some names to the top of your list and eliminate others. It's part of the selection process, along with acquiring names through recommendations and referrals and getting estimates. The most specific source of this information is in the detailed professional entries that follow. Each listing has a section entitled "Qualifications," which covers the requirements, from apprenticeships to state licenses, that a contractor needs to perform the professional service. But there are other, more general, sources.

One is the Better Business Bureau. You can write their national headquarters for the address and phone number of the branch nearest you. The Better Business Bureau keeps records on many individual firms. They can tell you if the way a company conducts business produces a lot of consumer complaints and how typical consumers' problems have been resolved.

The Better Business Bureau is a particularly good source of information on deceptive advertising and mail fraud. Talk to your postmaster on this subject also. The bureau has kept track of fraud through the mail since the 1800s when "Complete Sewing Machines for 25 Cents" turned out to be twelve needles, and a "Bona fide, steel-engraved portrait of General Grant," also for a quarter, turned out to be a 1-cent stamp with Grant's face on it. (You might be interested in their pamphlet on advertising practices. It covers standards for products and services, and includes examples of some of the worst pitfalls. If you encounter untrue or inaccurate advertising claims, do your part and report them to the National Advertising Division (NAD) of the Better Business Bureau [845 Third Ave., New York, NY 10022].)

The bureau doesn't provide legal advice or recommend one contractor over another, and they can't intervene over questions of price. But they should be able to help you eliminate substandard contractors.

There's another good general source, right in the back of this book. It's the appendix of "Consumer Information Sources." This list has federal, state, county, and city consumer agencies that can provide a lot of valuable information. Use this source in addition to the particulars under each professional entry.

No matter what contractor you're dealing with, some branch of the government or some consumer agency is interested. They are in a position to recognize the problems you have and to respond with the kind of information you need.

In many areas, consumer-protection agencies are a division of the town or county attorney's office. Larger cities tend to have more autonomous consumer agencies. In any case, they are not hard to get hold of. If my list doesn't pinpoint the right one for you, pick up your phone and start calling your local officials. Try the county clerk, the building department, the supervisor's or the mayor's office, and the county courthouse until you are steered to the appropriate local agency that can handle your request.

One piece of information in particular is worth tracking down. It is the local requirements, if any, for home contractors. In some areas, builders, plumbers, and others may not need to pass an exam, or to be certified, or to carry insurance, or anything else. That's worth knowing. It's not great news, but at least you'll know where you stand.

However, in many areas, contractors and other home professionals must be licensed in order to do business, even though the license is not a guarantee of good work. It may be as hard to get as a fishing license or it may signify a reliable record of local service. It pays to find out what the license means.

You can verify the length of a local business's practice by checking the date of the company's registration. These records are kept at county record offices (call the county clerk). The Better Business Bureau should be able to give you this information also.

Evaluating Informal Agreements and Formal Contracts

If you are looking for definitive, expert opinions on contract law, consult an attorney. For professional work costing more than you make in two weeks, I suggest you protect yourself by having an attorney check any contract before you sign.

Elaborate contracts with pages of fine print are not required for every job. They are usually reserved for large projects where the total cost is divided into several payments, and, of course, on all work where financing (a loan or extended time payments) is provided along with the professional service.

Informal agreements can serve for straightforward jobs that are limited in scope, time, and cost. A payment of $1,000 should be considered the upper limit for an informal agreement. The agreement can be typed in letter form; it should outline the work and should be agreed to by both parties. It is not uncommon for contractors to submit estimates that become agreements with the addition of your signature. These estimate-contracts may contain most or all of the information a good agreement should contain. But, for several reasons, I advise you not to sign this kind of contract.

I am naturally wary of any agreement drawn up by only one of the interested parties. The language may be fair, but the idea doesn't seem fair. You should participate in the contract process, and this will help set the tone of your relationship with the professional. You are going to be evaluating his work and paying for the results. I suggest that you tell the contractor you will draw up the agreement (even if most of the language you plan to use comes from his estimate). This will put the contractor through one final test.

If the professional balks at this suggestion, if it has to be *his* contract or none at all, make it none at all. Why should a professional object to your version of the agreement if it includes all the pertinent details of his estimate? He will probably object because your agreement has closed a loophole he wants as an escape hatch. Well, you don't want to hire someone who's looking for a way out before he even gets in the door.

Here are the basics of an informal agreement: it should start with a paragraph, written in your own words, that identifies the document, its purpose and its scope. For example, "This letter is to serve as an agreement between [your name and address] and [the contractor's name and address] with regard to the work of reroofing the single-family house at [your address, county, lot or plot number off the tax rolls or other identification]."

The body of the agreement can take many forms. Among the least complicated is a point-by-point outline covering the following:

1. A description of the work area, establishing boundaries, specific exclusions, and other considerations—for example, that a hedge beneath the wall to be painted must be protected during the job.

2. A description of the work itself, covering each stage from start to finish. For example, that the existing shingles will be removed, new tarpaper laid down, drip-edge and flashing replaced, new shingles laid, and new gutters and leaders installed. You can't be too specific.

3. A description of the materials, called the specifications, that qualifies words like shingles, gutters, and tarpaper. Trade names, weights, dimensions, color, style, configuration, and all other identifying characteristics should be listed.

4. Guarantees of product life and performance should also be spelled out. If a home-improvement job includes the installation of a dishwasher, for example, the manufacturer's guarantee should be passed on to you, and it should be mentioned in the agreement. Don't leave any loose ends.

5. The contractor should guarantee his liability for personal injury and property damage on the job. You ask if he has insurance. He says yes. You ask if he'll put it in the agreement. He says it's not necessary. You say good-bye.

6. A date on which the job will start and one on which it will finish should be included with the phrase "the dates are of the essence of the contract." This gives you more legal leverage if the job lags to the point where you wind up in court.

7. The total cost and the method of payment should be detailed. Follow this simple guideline: minimize the first payment and maximize the final one. On jobs where a lot of expensive materials must be ordered up front it may be only fair to provide some money up front, too. Limit it to 15 percent of the total price, and reserve at least as much, preferably 20 to 25 percent, as a final payment made after all work is completed, all rubbish is removed, and the work area is left "broom clean."

These are the basics of every contract, big or small. There are two specialized provisions you should know about: a Waiver of Mechanic's Lien Rights and Right of Refusal. The Waiver is a document that states that subcontractors give up their right to collect from you any money the general contractor owes them. It should be supplied at the end of every job where a general contractor uses subcontractors to complete a portion of the work. The Right of Refusal allows you to reject a subcontractor whose performance record is inadequate.

Complex work may have to be outlined in a complex document with special provisions governing peculiarities of a particular profession. That's why you need an attorney. Pay particular attention to language that describes financing arrangements. Some states have "plain language" laws so that true costs can't be buried in "parties of the first part," and "scheduled properties accruing to the lessee." Check the "Consumer Information Sources" index for consumer banking agencies. They can tell you the standards of financial contract language in your area.

Some states also have cooling-off periods, that is, a short period of time after you sign a contract when you can rethink the proposition and back out. Call your local consumer protection agency or district attorney's office in rural areas on this.

Solving Grievances

Of all the operations in the Primer, this is the most difficult. It can be more difficult than going to court, though sometimes that's the only answer. All the smart consumer practices of getting recommendations, checking references, writing protective agreements, and more are intended to keep you out of this quagmire.

Legalities are only part of the problem. You can also have problems because your mom and dad raised you to be polite, tactful, and sociable. If you have grown up with an aversion to personal confrontations, you could be in big trouble. Suppose the deck you contracted for should have been completed a week ago. You called the builder all week long, but his wife sidestepped your questions: he's out; he's sick; he'll call you; he'll be there tomorrow. You don't have the stomach to get abrasive over the phone with a woman you've never met; after all, she sounds very warm and sincere.

The deck is now two weeks late, and you're getting abrasive with everyone because you're supposed to take your kids camping next month—if the deck is done by then. The wood, the nails, and the stain are at the job site. The weather is good. Everything is ready—the footings are poured; the girders are in place. Everything is ready, that is, except the builder.

He is now three weeks late on a job that should have lasted fourteen days. You threaten to withhold final payment. You threaten to sue. Nothing happens. The unfinished deck complicates your days and invades your dreams. Is there any way out from under?

You can always go to court, but that's the extreme answer. This course of action will probably net you about half the money you need to finish the job a month late. Not a stunning alternative.

Even if you do go to court, you may not get very far unless a completion date is in your contract. You should add another helpful provision to your contract as well. It should state that if the job is interrupted for an unreasonable time (this must be specified and will depend on the complexity and normal duration of the project) you have the right to apply the unpaid portion of the contract amount toward alternative means of completing the work. This is the best out you can ask for. It is one reason for leaving a large final payment; it is also a provision that no contractor likes. This provision keeps them from juggling jobs to suit their needs instead of running your job to suit your needs.

Beyond this legal leverage, try to negotiate. Be logical. Communicate with a cool head. If the work has stopped or is proceeding in a disastrous fashion that is inconsistent with your contract, try to establish a new and realistic goal. Offer an accommodation along with the financial carrot of the final payment. You may get results.

Never offer to pay off the job. Never offer to pay off a subcontractor or a material supplier. *Never* give away your ultimate leverage—

money. Try an accommodation of time: "Look, I know the deck is three weeks late according to the contract, but why don't we set a new completion date?" Better late than never, right? Maybe the builder needs to work evenings or Sundays. Try to understand his problem—you're not being philanthropic, it's in your own interest.

Personal negotiation may not work. You may have had so many disagreements with the contractor that communication is fruitless. The work may be so poor, such a butcher job, that meeting the professional halfway would still leave you in a hole. If you can't get anywhere, try third-party negotiation. This process can be included in a contract as well. You can go to the Better Business Bureau, the grievance committee of the professional's society or trade association, an industry arbitration panel (specific organizations are listed with the professional entries they cover), and, finally, a consumer-protection association. Many offer mediation services.

But this may not work either. For all your efforts of careful selection, you may have picked the one well driller in a thousand who can find anything but water. It happens. But if you follow the Primer guidelines and use the entries carefully, you will minimize your risks.

Principles for the Home Consumer

TRUST YOUR INSTINCTS

Think of the people you know—some are easy to get along with; some are impossible. Some are honest and industrious; others are dishonest and lazy. A cross section of home contractors sorts out the same way—they're people too. An association with some trade group, a license to practice, or an elaborate advertisement doesn't offer foolproof assurances about a person's work. Sorting through recommendations will help, but don't underestimate your personal instincts or your first impressions. Use your common sense when dealing with contractors; it's valuable.

COMPETITION IS HEALTHY

You're planning to sign up AAA Plumbing because they are first in the phone book? You're satisfied with one quote for installing your water-softening system? Don't be; open it up a little. Let some other folks have a chance. It's the American way—a little healthy competition will keep all those home professionals on their toes. Get at least three estimates for every job. Shop around and let the contractors know you're doing it. You'll be surprised how negotiable some of those rock-bottom prices can become.

HESITATE UNDER PRESSURE

No, you won't find this principle in *The Power of Positive Thinking*, but there are times when caution is called for in the real world. If a carpenter presses you to sign on the spot, hesitate. If a repairman offers a special one-day deal on parts or materials left over from another job, hesitate. If the home contractor can only start work immediately, and doesn't have time to talk about licenses or insurance or satisfied customers, hesitate. If you are pressed to make a decision about any deal that seems too good to be true, hesitate. Speculate on the Irish Sweepstakes, not on the place where you live.

REMEMBER, YOU'RE THE SUPPLY, THEY'RE THE DEMAND

This is difficult to remember because usually it's the other way around: ordinarily you provide the demand for a car or a quart of milk and the company offers the supply. But now you're the company and you've got the job to offer. Don't underestimate the power this gives you. Take a look through the phone book. There are a lot of contractors, and they all need to keep working. Be picky.

DON'T BE A HOME GUINEA PIG

Degrees and licenses are valuable, but a contractor's experience is the crucial bottom line. Credentials may indicate that the job should work out all right. But the contractor's record tells you it already has—and the more times it has, the better. Everyone has to get experience somewhere. A U.S. Army ad says, "We don't ask for experience, we give it." Terrific, but you're not the U.S. Army. Let contractors get their experience in apprentice programs and internships, not on your furnace or foundation. Insist on references and check them carefully. If the professional can't convince you he has had success with jobs similar to the one you have in mind, talk to someone who can.

LISTEN AND YOU SHOULD UNDERSTAND

Sure, there are many technical terms in home-consumer fields. All professionals use them as communications shortcuts and to feel secure when they talk to one another. But technical jargon is no substitute for results. You're paying for high-quality work not high-quality language. It's the classic joke: only the pharmacist can decipher the doctor's handwriting. But it's no joke when you can't understand the fine print on a home-improvement contract. You're the client. You're paying the bill, and that entitles you to ask questions. If you don't understand the technical answers, ask again. If you can't get an explanation that makes sense, ask someone else.

GET IT IN WRITING

It's so simple, so obvious; you know you should do it, but a lot of people don't. Prices agreed to with a handshake are meaningless. Promises that are spoken but not written down are empty. Try taking your case to court without a written contract. Big jobs will require more legal paperwork than small repairs, but before any money is paid, get up a letter of agreement outlining the work, service, measurable result, names, addresses, amount of time and money allotted, and method of payment (and always keep *at least* 15 percent for a little leverage as a final payment). With the security of a contract, you will have something to fall back on.

PART II:

HOME CONTRACTORS

Air-conditioning Contractors

Air conditioning was once a luxury. Not anymore. The demand for cooling now consumes about 23 percent of all the energy used at home, compared to 28 percent for space heating. Air conditioning is one of the most desired features in a new home, and among the most cost-effective home improvements you can make. (You'll get your money back if you sell.) Central air systems that condition every room and individual appliances that cool specific areas both work on the same principle. You should know something about how air conditioning works because if you don't, and the contractor can tell you don't, you may be in for a hustle.

Here are the basics: a liquid refrigerant (usually Freon) is pumped through two bundles of pipes by a compressor. Freon in the pipe bundle facing outside the home (called the condenser coil) takes the form of a hot, high-pressure gas that gives up heat. As it passes through an expansion valve into the pipe bundle facing inside the home (called the evaporator coil), the Freon changes into a cool, low-pressure gas that absorbs heat. The compressor keeps pumping the Freon through the pipes so it expands and contracts, picks up and gives up heat, in a continuous cycle.

SERVICES

Some air conditioners are installed by air-conditioning specialists. Most, particularly central or whole-house systems, are installed by general heating and cooling contractors. Room units may require professional installation if they are mounted through the wall, but you should be able to install window air conditioners by yourself.

When you buy room air conditioners you'll deal with an appliance salesman. When you buy central units you'll purchase them through your contractor. In both cases the professionals should provide accurate information about the unit's size and efficiency.

Capacity is the number of British thermal units (BTUs) of heat that can be removed in an hour. Some salesmen will specify size in tons of cooling (1 ton of cooling equals 12,000 BTUs), but the appliance should be stamped with a BTU rating. Horsepower and wattage ratings do not describe cooling capacity.

Efficiency is now expressed by an energy efficiency rating (EER) that, by law, must appear on all air conditioners. It provides information about operating costs, which, on a national average, usually exceed the purchase price of your system after two to three years of operation.

Be wary of salesmen or contractors who push you toward larger and larger capacity—you don't need an air conditioner that will keep everything cool during the hottest day on record. For a rough check on their recommendations for room conditioners use this guide: 12,000 BTUs (1 ton) of cooling capacity per 500 sq. ft. of floor space. For a more accurate check, use the WHILE formula. Here's how it works:

W=room width; H=room height; I=insulation factor (substitute the number 10 if the area is covered by an insulated, ventilated attic or another cool apartment, and the number 18 for a top-floor apartment or area with no insulation or vented space above); L=room length; E=exposure factor (substitute the number 16 if the longest room or house dimension faces north, 17 if it faces east, 18 for south, and 20 for west).

To use the formula substitute the appropriate numbers, multiply as shown below, and divide by 60. The answer is the number of BTUs of cooling capacity per hour you need.

Example: for a 15 x 20 ft. room with 8 ft. ceilings, insulated and vented above, with the longest wall facing south.

$$W \times H \times I \times L \times E \quad \text{(subtotal)} \quad \div 60 = \text{BTUs required}$$
$$15 \times 8 \times 10 \times 20 \times 18 \quad \text{(432,000)} \quad \div 60 = 7,200$$

In most cases, this estimate is as good or better than the one a salesman will make. But for central systems (or if you call in a contractor to install and balance several room units), capacity should be matched to the cooling load of your home. This figure is arrived at by determining how many people may normally occupy the space, the total wattage of electrical equipment in the area, and other hairsplitting details. You can compare the thoroughness of your contractor's investigation with the procedures outlined on the Cooling Load Estimate Form, available from the Association of Home Appliance Manufacturers (AHAM, 20 N. Wacker Dr., Chicago, IL 60606).

Don't buy any air-conditioning equipment that does not have an EnergyGuide label. This label and not the promises of a salesman or contractor tells how much the unit will cost to run; it has a chart on which you can figure out your annual electricity costs. The top EER rating is 11.6—the higher the number the more efficient the air conditioner. The EnergyGuide label compares the EER for the appliance you're looking at to the least and most efficient models on the market.

QUALIFICATIONS

At the top of the professional ladder is the engineer. He will design a cooling system for your home and supervise its installation. He will be expensive, and his service is probably unnecessary. The American Society of Heating, Refrigeration and Air-Conditioning Engineers (ASHRAE, 1791 Tullie Circle NE, Atlanta, Ga. 30329) will provide the name of an engineer if you want one. They have some 30,000 members and 125 local groups. (ASHRAE has 87 technical committees that establish industry-wide standards in eleven different areas; for example, they have a panel on Heating, Ventilating, and Air-Conditioning [HVAC] Systems, and on HVAC Equipment. You can write ASHRAE for their guidelines on calculating heating and cooling loads, interior-air quality, requirements for duct construction, insulation, and other standards.)

Many heating and cooling contractors employ an engineer—he is the guy who wanders through your home in work boots and clean khakis noting the minute details of window size, insulation, and construction. He has all the signs of a professional with a technical degree (he must know what he's doing, right?), so most homeowners don't ask him any questions. But this is the stage at which all the details of the system are being planned. Ask the engineer every question you can think of about the size and noise of the system the contractor wants to install; also ask about condensation, operating costs, and small home-improvement projects like caulking or installing awnings, which will make the air-conditioning system more effective.

Some contractors, particularly those working on straightforward residential jobs, may compute cooling loads and design air-conditioning systems without the help of an engineer. This takes a lot of experience. Professionals affiliated with the Airconditioning Contractors of America (ACA, 1228 17th St. NW, Washington, DC 20036) should have the expertise to size and install central units, although the ACA requires only one year of experience for membership (some local chapters specify two years).

There are many air-conditioning options, including heat pumps (particularly effective in mild climates where heating and cooling loads are roughly equal), and water-cooled systems. Your equipment can be mounted in a cellar, crawl space, or attic; it can be in a single package or split inside and outside the home. Deal with contractors who can explain the advantages of a specific system for your home, not just that it's the best system around.

PROFESSIONAL PRACTICES

A salesman's job is to sell. Some try to twist your arm; others present the facts. At a minimum, you should see and hear about the BTU-per-hour rating and the EER label. But expect the sale to be pitched toward high cooling capacity. You may be asked questions that "discover" extra heat loads. Is the air-conditioned room next to a hot kitchen or occasionally used for summer parties where you pack a lot of people in?

Bigger is not necessarily better. An air conditioner with more capacity than you need will cool the area quickly and then shut off. A properly sized unit will run longer, probably keeping inside temperature more uniform; it will also dry out the air more effectively. If you need to, you can always use a small room fan to increase the range of your air conditioner.

Most companies offer one-year warranties on parts and labor for room air conditioners and five years on the air-sealed components. The price of extending protection in a service contract varies widely (by almost 50 percent among the major chains like Sears, J. C. Penney, and Montgomery Ward). If you rent your home, check your lease—you may find a clause that prohibits any projections from the building, including air conditioners. Also, you have to match the wiring on the air conditioner; most are 110-volt that can be plugged into a 15-amp branch circuit, but some are 220-volt. The two are not interchangeable.

Some landlords may levy a surcharge for cooling that is added to your operating costs. One apartment dweller who called in to my weekly radio show in New York said she had been paying for "special" 220-volt wiring for eight years. After she checked, it turned out that her air conditioner was a standard 110-volt model that could plug into any wall outlet. Contact the manufacturer if you have any questions about required voltage.

If you live in a house and you're installing a central system, the contractors should provide a written estimate including dates for starting and finishing the work; the name, type, size, capacity, price, and efficiency of the equipment; the size and type of ductwork; the type of duct insulation and its R-Value (the material's resistance to transmitting heat). Ask to see a copy of the Cooling Load Form, and compare it to the AHAM form. As always, ask for references from former clients, including a few who can tell you about long-term servicing.

Standard warranties on central systems run one year on parts and labor, with four-year coverage on the compressor. Most contractors will make one free service call to fine-tune the system. Experienced contractors should also be able to make recommendations for the complete conditioning of the air, *i.e.*, installing an electronic air cleaner (particularly valuable if someone in the house has allergies) or a humidity control system.

When a new central or room air conditioner breaks down, go back to the contractor or the retailer/installer where you bought it for service. This is essential if the unit is under warranty. On older units, when you can't get help from or find the installer, choose a factory-authorized service company. Check this frequently misused Yellow Pages listing (Factory Parts, for instance, is not Factory-Authorized Service) with the manufacturer.

For all but emergency repairs, verify the serviceman's diagnosis and suggested solution with the manufacturer as well. Some of the most common, easily repaired problems have symptoms similar to one of the worst—a dying or dead compressor. If, despite all kinds of problems and delays, your air conditioner will produce some cool air and you do not hear the dull clunking and clanking of a bad compressor, chances are that low Freon levels (not enough refrigerant, possibly from a slow leak) or malfunctioning thermostat controls are at fault.

Check your owner's manual for elementary troubleshooting advice first, then look for factory-authorized service and a second or third opinion if you hear that expedient and expensive diagnosis of a bad compressor.

EVALUATING WORK

It may be hard to plan ahead this carefully, but you will probably get better service and a better price for the job if the work is done in the fall or winter. And more contractors will be available. Of course, you want your air-conditioning system to be efficient. Check with your local or state energy departments and find out if your state requires minimum EER ratings. In New York, for example, new air conditioners under 6,000 BTUs must have a minimum EER of 8.7, as of January 1, 1981. Units over 6,000 BTUs must have an 8.7 EER. But remember that operating costs are most affected by thermostat settings. Every degree of cooling you can do without (bumping the thermostat from 78 to 79 degrees for instance, which I doubt that you'll feel) will save approximately 5 percent of your total cooling costs.

To evaluate specific room air conditioners, write Consumers Union (CU, 256 Washington St., Mt. Vernon, NY 10550), and ask for their ratings of high-efficiency units (5,000–5,300 BTU/hour with EERs of 7.5 or over, and 6,800–7,500 BTU/hour with EERs of 7.5 to 10.2. Friedrich Air Conditioning and Refrigeration has a model that's expensive to buy but cheap to run rated 10.2. CU regularly includes room air conditioners in their annual buying guide. They charge for reprints.

Beware of stores where you have trouble getting the details of warranty protection. Some retailers bury the warranty sheets in order to sell service contracts that may offer some duplicate protection. Major chains (including the now defunct Korvette's) have had trouble with the Federal Trade Commission because their warranty information was not properly displayed.

GRIEVANCES

Your first step should be to attempt mediation with the contractor. Then go to the appropriate professional society, if the contractor is affiliated. You can also contact an AHAM-sponsored group, the Major Appliance Consumer Action Panel (MACAP, 20 N. Wacker Dr., Chicago, IL 60606, 312-984-7610), which offers mediation services.

Some manufacturers maintain customer service centers for consumer information and handle complaints. Whirlpool has a twenty-four-hour, toll-free number (800-253-1301 or 800-632-2243, in Michigan) for general information, complaints, and referrals to nearby service centers. The Westinghouse Appliance Service can be reached toll-free (800-245-0600, or 800-242-0580 in Pennsylvania). General Electric can be contacted by writing to: Director of Customer Relations, General Electric Company, Major Appliance Group, Appliance Park, Louisville, KY 40225.

If you can't resolve the problem locally, bring the manufacturer into the picture. This may make your contractor more agreeable.

Arborists

Trees can increase the value of your property and save on energy costs by shading summer sun and breaking cold winter winds. But in countless subdivisions bulldozers run rampant, stripping and flattening the land, until every vacant building lot looks the same. This is to make surveys, access roads, drainage lines, gas pipes, water mains, and most other components of construction economical for the builder. But many of the same builders then turn around and spend a lot of money trucking in grass from the sod farm and trees from the nursery to make their new homes more attractive and salable. Sometimes this amounts to no more than a temporary sugar coating that stays green only until you close on the house.

New, young trees may survive with a lot of care and feeding. Mature trees that are red-tagged to remain untouched, but come away from construction scarred by truck wheels or bulldozer blades or buried in regraded topsoil, may be in trouble. You may have to call in an experienced arborist.

Over your term of ownership, trees can be threatened by a variety of diseases, by drought, and, in some areas, by leaf-eating gypsy moths. Hand spraying and other home remedies may help, but if they don't, and you are serious about saving your trees, an arborist is your last recourse.

SERVICES

An experienced, professional arborist should offer complete tree service. This includes inspecting and diagnosing the condition of your trees, recommending corrective procedures, and estimating their cost. The arborist will prune, spray, fertilize, transplant, and protect trees during construction; he will also cable-brace or reinforce structurally weakened trees, install lightning protection (copper cables), and remove trees.

Professional arborists should be able to evaluate a wooded lot or a single tree according to the species, age, and structural characteristics. They can also explain disease or insect damage, soil conditions, and the possibility of transplant (called a transplant factor).

Qualified arborists may make appraisals of valuable existing trees; they can even provide written estimates of damage that can be used as testimony in court cases. Is this carrying their job a little too far? Not really. I once rented a house that had three large stumps in the front yard, close to the little-used country road. The rental agent said the stumps were once magnificent black walnut trees. One weekend, when the owners were away, they were stolen. According to the local police, it had taken less than 24 hours for the tree thieves to cut the black walnuts down, haul them to a mill, and have them cut into prime hardwood lumber worth about $3,000.

QUALIFICATIONS

Local experience is a primary criterion for hiring an arborist. A lengthy, local practice provides an arborist with a backlog of case histories, and familiarity with the types and incidence of regional tree diseases and with local codes regulating the application of pesticides.

Two organizations are active in this professional field. The National Arborist Association (NAA, 3537 Stratford Rd., Wantagh, NY 11793) represents practicing arborists who offer complete tree service. The association maintains standards for membership and educational programs in the field of arboriculture.

The American Society of Consulting Arborists (ASCA, 12 Lakeview Ave., Milltown, NJ 08850) requires applicants to be sponsored by two ASCA members or other knowledgeable professionals (like the local county agricultural agent), to submit educational and professional résumés, and to offer at least three consultation field reports. About 50 percent of their applicants are granted membership. ASCA currently looks for at least 5 years of field experience combined with educational training but they consider applicants carefully on a case-by-case basis.

Further recommendations and assurances of expertise may be obtained from the 3,000-member International Society of Arboriculture (ISA, 3 Lincoln Sq., Urbana, IL 61801), and the 2,500-member American Association of Nurserymen (AAN, 230 Southern Bldg., Washington, DC 20005), if the nursery professional has had experience with big trees, not just with lawns and gardens.

In about 15 states a certification exam is required for practicing arborists. Contact your state department of agriculture or your county agricultural agent to find out if certification or a license is required in your area. In New Jersey, for example, arborists must pass a full-day exam, half in the field and half in the classroom, to receive the title of Certified Tree Expert.

PROFESSIONAL PRACTICES

Make sure the professional arborist carries personal liability and property-damage insurance; you should get a guarantee of his coverage in any contract or agreement. After a consultation and field inspection to diagnose conditions, an arborist should present detailed recommendations for corrective treatment, including the name and chemical content of any pesticides that will be used, with price estimates. The use of pesticides is, with good reason, a sensitive issue. Be careful what you allow the arborist to use.

Structural or chemical treatment of big trees should be carried out in the safest possible circumstances. Clear the immediate area during tree removal. Arborists or the field technicians who work for them should forewarn you of spraying operations and recommend protective measures. Your next-door neighbor may have a legal case if his property is covered with a chemical mist from your spraying.

EVALUATING WORK

Check for membership in the National Arborist Association or the American Society of Consulting Arborists. You can obtain their membership directories for free. Also inquire about current state certification and licensing requirements. In addition to professional affiliations and recommendations from other clients (particularly about long-term care and results), talk to your county agricultural agent—every county has one. And expect him to give you three names, not to recommend only one arborist.

GRIEVANCES

Complaints about affiliated members should be directed to the grievance committees of either the NAA or ASCA. Concerns about specific treatments and pesticides should be referred to your county agent, the local health department, and the Environmental Protection Agency (EPA, Office of Pesticide Programs, Washington, DC 20460), which regulates, evaluates, and registers pesticides. For comparison purposes (and to let the arborist know that you know at least a little about trees) write for information on tree types, regional characteristics, and tree diseases to the Forest Service (U.S. Department of Agriculture, 12th St. and Independence Ave. SW, Washington, DC 20250).

Asphalt Pavers

A survey prepared jointly by the Department of Housing and Urban Development and the Federal Trade Commission found that close to 8 percent of new homeowners had a problem with their driveways. More disturbing was the news that only 20 percent of these complaints were resolved by the builder. What about the other 80 percent? These driveways became old before their time, and prime candidates for one of the most unregulated, ripoff-prone fields of home improvement.

SERVICES

Residential driveway construction, repair, and maintenance may be handled by three different trades depending on the materials the driveway is made of. For crushed stone or gravel, which compresses into the soil under traffic and has to be replaced periodically, you should contact a general landscaper (see page 75); for concrete drives, a mason (see page 91). But for asphalt drives (also called blacktop drives), which are by far the most common today, you'll need an asphalt-paving contractor.

The contractor should be able to clear and grade the site, prepare a firm driveway base, as well as haul in, place, and roll the asphalt surface layers. Some paving contractors may be able to provide only one of the three different types of asphalt driveway treatments.

A Cold Mix Application combines asphalt and aggregate (small stone) and should be applied in layers that are at least 1 in. thick. This method is commonly used for patching work, a do-it-yourself kind of job requiring only a few bags of premixed material that is available at most building-supply outlets and lumberyards. It can be dumped into potholes, then tamped and rolled. You can even cover the patch area with a smooth piece of plywood, and compact it by driving your car back and forth over the wood.

A Surface Treatment, also called a wearing course, is a 1-in.-thick coating of liquid asphalt that is covered with mineral aggregates. It has limited durability, is watertight only to light traffic, and should not be applied unless you already have a firm and fully prepared driveway base.

A Hot Mix Application, also called hot top, is the most durable. Aggregate and asphalt, batched together at an asphalt plant, is applied in 1-in. thick (or thicker) layers while it is hot. The more layers the contractor applies, the better. This is the kind of work that cuts a three-lane highway down to one lane in the summer. Hot Mix does not require curing time and may need resurfacing only at seven-to ten-year intervals, depending on local weather and traffic.

Pay particularly close attention to contractors who sell patching and resurfacing services. Many cases have been documented by the Better Business Bureau and consumer protection agencies of resurfacing that was accomplished with several gallons of used engine oil. Incredible? You bet. But it looks smooth, glossy, and very much like an asphalt coating as it goes down. Of course, the oil does absolutely no good and will probably wash away in streaks during the first rain. The oil also creates both a safety hazard and a pollution problem.

QUALIFICATIONS

Reputable contractors, even when they're desperate for work, are not likely to cruise around the neighborhood with a few gallons of "asphaltlike" material in the back of their station wagon. If you are solicited this way, and offered a break (which may break your leg and your checkbook) on materials left over from a job down the street, beware. Ask to see the job, and talk to the homeowner. Ask for the names of clients who had work done several weeks and months ago. If the contractor wants a substantial portion of the price up front, refuse. Find another contractor. You can afford to be picky—the Chamber of Commerce figures that in a metropolitan area with a population of one million, there are, on average, 124 firms doing driveway work.

You don't necessarily need a professional paver for light patching jobs. If you can't handle them yourself, a general handyman should be able to. But for extensive repairs (10 percent or more of the driveway surface), resurfacing, or new driveway construction, you will need a contractor who has a dump truck, a roller, and a crew of workers. Don't accept hand rolling (using a hand-propelled, tennis court-type roller) on anything but minor patches.

Affiliation with the National Asphalt Pavement Association (NAPA, 6811 Kenilworth Ave., Riverdale, MD 20840) or a state branch of that group is a plus for any contractor. But client recommendations and the length of local business practice are crucial in this unregulated field.

PROFESSIONAL PRACTICES

After asking three or more contractors for bids, compare how thoroughly each one inspects the site. You can't get a realistic estimate over the phone or from a look at the site. It's not enough. A good contract must include specific details that can be determined only after basic information like soil composition and drainage characteristics has been evaluated. Each site is a little different. Weed-filled sites may require a soil sterilant. Sloping sites may require drains.

A good contract should include the type and thickness of the driveway base, thickness of the surface asphalt, the exact finished dimensions, starting and finishing dates, and a limited warranty. It must specify the job price, and permit you to reserve at least 15 percent as a final payment.

On new driveway construction, the contractor must clear away soft topsoil and roll the firm subsoil. A 6,000-lb. roller is adequate. On unstable soils, a 3- to 5-in.-thick subbase of crusher-run stone or bank-run gravel (both are relatively low cost) should be laid for stability and durability. You could lay a beautiful asphalt drive right over your lawn. But without adequate preparation of a firm base, it wouldn't last very long.

Asphalt should ideally be applied in layers with roughly two-thirds of the total thickness laid first as a binder course (with larger aggregate), and one-third laid on top—the wearing course. For adequate drainage, the driveway should slope away from your house or garage and toward the street about 2 in. downhill for every 10 linear ft. that is laid. Additional drains may be required on hilly sites.

To resurface existing asphalt drives that have deteriorated, all soft, spongy areas should be removed down to a firm base. Weeds should be chemically treated, and drains cleared if necessary. The new surface layer of asphalt should be close to 1 in. thick to be durable. And asphalt for new driveways or resurfacing work should never be put down in rain, snow, or below-freezing temperatures.

Surface sealing, sometimes called renewing asphalt, is the specialty of fly-by-nighters. Insist on a contract (or at least an informal agreement) even for this easy, relatively low-cost work. It should name the sealer that will be used—either a quality bituminous, water-emulsion type, or a coal-tar sealer for added protection against oil and gasoline. On sloping drives, sharp sand should be added to increase traction.

EVALUATING WORK

Does your driveway need to be resurfaced? Try this simple test on a hot, sunny day. Pour a bucket of water on the driveway. After the surface water has evaporated, the pavement will still look darker where the water landed if a significant amount has seeped into the blacktop. This water infiltration causes deterioration, which should be prevented by sealing the surface. If the water evaporates evenly, and no dark area remains, you don't need a sealer.

Check the thoroughness of subgrade preparation on new work. The ground should be compacted, particularly if you anticipate heavy loads from a garbage or oil truck. The best way to do this is with a vibrating power roller. This action is not possible with hand rollers.

You should also verify the contractor's work. No, you don't have to lean over his shoulder; wait until he knocks off for the day. Rip-offs like this have been documented: the contract specifies 2½ in. of asphalt but less than ½ in. is actually put down.

GRIEVANCES

In this unregulated field you have only the standard grievance channels, *i.e.,* a local licensing board that puts the stamp of approval on home-improvement contractors, a local Better Business Bureau, a trade association (if the contractor is a member), a consumer-protection agency, and, finally, into court with a copy of your contract. Many of the most successful fly-by-nighters, however, won't have a license; they won't have a record with the Better Business Bureau or with a local consumer agency either. Many move from town to town, strike fast, and move on before anyone can catch up with them.

Hire contractors who have been around for a while, and withhold enough of the total job price (at least 15 percent) to discourage any contractor from taking construction shortcuts or from leaving the job unfinished.

You can write the Asphalt Institute (AI, Asphalt Institute Bldg., College Park, MD 20740) for model-job specifications, and the National Asphalt Pavement Association for a copy of their "Consumer's Fact Sheet for Hot-Mix Asphalt Driveways."

Basement Waterproofers

If a water pipe breaks, chances are you'll attend to the problem immediately, but the effects of a damp basement are not immediately apparent. The moving parts of your power tools in the basement shop won't solidify with rust overnight. It takes time.

Your home insurance will probably cover the sudden and accidental damage from a burst pipe. But I doubt it will cover long-term deterioration from seepage, foundation leaks, or severe condensation, which can be just as bad.

A Department of Housing and Urban Development/Federal Trade Commission study found that 7 percent of new homeowners across the country reported problems with wet basements. Sounds like a reasonable percentage? It's not—there is no excuse for it. On new construction, when the exterior surfaces of foundation walls are accessible, complete and long-lasting waterproofing is an easy, straightforward process. It only gets difficult and expensive after the fact, after excavated dirt is backfilled against the foundation, and landscaping is completed.

Is there a simple, relatively inexpensive way to waterproof existing foundations? No. If you get what I call a quick and dirty answer, it will be the wrong answer. There is no miracle product or process that can redo the waterproofing job a builder or mason should have done during construction.

SERVICES

You don't have to have water pouring through the foundation to have a wet basement. So before you pull out the Yellow Pages pin down the source of the water. It's not that difficult to do.

I like to start small, invest a little money and a little time on an optimistic diagnosis. If the problem turns out to be serious (and it frequently does) I haven't lost much. It just doesn't make sense to start with the most disruptive, expensive solution, which, in this case, is calling in an excavator to expose the foundation and start from scratch.

There are two easy ways to find out if the wetness in your basement is from a leak or from condensation. On an average day, the kind of day when the walls are normally wet, attach a small pocket mirror to the inside of the foundation wall. Dry a small area first (a hair dryer works nicely), then stick the mirror in place (a large wad of bubble gum will do it). Wait twenty-four hours. If the mirror surface facing you is foggy, the problem is condensation. If it's clear, there's a leak. Why? Because temperature variations on the inside and outside of the foundation wall work just like a warm front meeting a cold front on the weather map: they meet, moisture in the air condenses (and there is usually plenty of moisture in basement air), you get clouds (a foggy mirror), and rain (condensation).

You can make another, even more reliable test by taping a hand-size piece of aluminum foil against the inside foundation overnight. Again, dry the area first so the tape will adhere (duct tape works well). Moisture on the surface of the foil indicates condensation. The area beneath the patch should be dry if the tape has kept out the wet air. But moisture beneath the foil indicates a leak. And if the foil has swelled and split open from water pressure, go immediately to the Yellow Pages and look under Canoes —you'll need one.

For condensation problems, the best answer is more ventilation and less humidity. Shop around for a dehumidifier. You can get ratings from *Consumer Reports* magazine. Or call in several heating and cooling contractors for estimates on exhaust fans and a duct system. It may even pay to dump a small amount of conditioned air from a central cooling system into the basement.

Small, isolated leaks and extremely slow seepage may be possible to correct from inside the basement. A professional waterproofer or a good mason might use a hydraulic cement (it's very watertight and swells slightly as it dries to fill up cracks and joints completely) to stop minor problems. A water-resistant paint (there's no such thing as a waterproof paint) may be enough to stop more widespread but very minimal seepage. A contractor should specify either powder or premixed cement-based paints for this job. Application can be made only after pointing the wall, an operation where all cracks and crevices are cleaned and refilled with mortar, or better yet, hydraulic cement.

Working on the outside—that's where you have to work to stop major leaks—involves reexcavating the foundation. The waterproofer will need a back-hoe operated with a light touch. It should be possible to save shrubs and small trees next to the house by lifting them and their root bundles with the back-hoe bucket.

There are many ways to waterproof a foundation after the wall is exposed. A thick, troweled-on asphalt coating (the masonry will have to be cleaned first), covered with thick, polyethylene sheeting (stretched from ground level, down the wall, across the joint between foundation and footing to a gravel-lined trench fitted with drain tile or perforated pipe), will do the job nicely. More sophisticated semirigid, asphalt-panel membranes may be used, some of which incorporate insulation. If you reduce the temperature variation on either side of the foundation wall you can help cure condensation problems at the same time.

QUALIFICATIONS

Don't bother looking for a waterproofer's association or state waterproofing certification. This is an unregulated specialty trade. Waterproofing should be done by masons as they complete the foundation. But as construction costs increase, waterproofing may be done quickly, and, worse yet, applied on house foundations that have little chance of staying dry because they are built on poor sites.

When houses were few and far between, only good, naturally formed sites were selected, like small hills and knolls that drained well. But now, in order to save money, natural sites are bulldozed so that homes can be mass-produced. Natural run-off gullies are filled in, streams diverted, and natural springs are buried under 6 ft. of fresh fill. If the foundation is in the path of a natural run-off, your basement may eventually get wet no matter how well the foundation is waterproofed.

Finding the source of groundwater can be difficult. It takes a solid knowledge of local soil conditions, of the water table (that's the level at which water naturally rests in the ground), of drainage characteristics, and, hopefully, a local contractor's memory of what the site looked like before it was developed.

PROFESSIONAL PRACTICES

There is no way that a professional waterproofer can take a quick look at your basement walls and know whether the water is coming from a leak or condensation, unless it's coming through like Niagara Falls. And a waterproofer who sells only one kind of service may tend to recommend that service as the best solution—no matter where the water is coming from.

In many cases, water comes from the roof. Rain goes into the gutters, down the leaders, and out onto the ground. That's the problem. Water should be directed into underground drains that carry it away from the house or it will travel down the foundation wall and into the basement. The remedy may involve only a moderate amount of regrading so that earth slopes away from the house, along with the installation of inexpensive plastic pipe to carry the water away.

A consumer's group called Washington Consumer's Checkbook (WCC) set up a controlled experiment with a test basement. It had wet conditions that several independent experts agreed could be solved simply for about $300 by regrading and extending the downspouts away from the foundation. Incredibly, nine out of ten waterproofing firms that submitted estimates for this test-case job recommended work costing from $1,200 to $2,000. This report, including three other studies, is available for $5.65 from WCC, 1518 K St., Suite 406, Washington, DC 20005.

This should be all the warning you need. But even if you have an iron-clad contract with complete specifications, prices, dates, insurance, and a guarantee, it may all be for the wrong job. Remember, start small, find out what kind of water you've got and where it's coming from before you opt for the expensive waterproofing job.

EVALUATING WORK

Watch out for contractors offering services described as clay injection, pressure pumping, or sodium-bentonite treatment. The idea with all three is to pump a claylike material into the ground along the foundation; somehow it will spread along the masonry wall and seal out water. Now that would be a neat trick.

No material, claylike or otherwise, can be selectively guided through dirt, tree roots, gravel, and rocks to settle evenly against a masonry wall. As for sodium bentonite: sodium is a soft, silvery-white metal that is very reactive, that is, it reacts with water to form sodium hydroxide and hydrogen gas; bentonite is a claylike material very similar to Fuller's Earth, which is used to absorb oil and grease. Can you figure it out? It makes no sense for waterproofing foundations. The Better Business Bureau has reported, "Clay injection, widely advertised over the last few years, has resulted in a substantial number of complaints." *Consumer Reports* magazine judged the process as useless. (Write Consumers Union, Reader's Service, 256 Washington St., Mt. Vernon, NY 10550, for an article entitled, "Basement Waterproofing: Facing The Facts." There is a charge for reprints.)

GRIEVANCES

See the Primer for guidelines on unregulated home services. It is crucial that you investigate a waterproofing contractor's reputation for honesty as well as expertise. If problems develop, get in touch with local consumer protection agencies quickly.

I hear from a lot of homeowners on my weekly radio program, and too many of them report that they have a grievance, and a contract, but can't find the company. It's too damn easy to fold up a company to avoid lawsuits, then open for business, the same business, under a new name. Check into the length of local business practice very carefully.

Carpenters

Of all the home professionals, a good carpenter is one of the hardest to track down. There are plenty of them around; that's not the problem. But there are so many kinds of carpenters with such a variety of special skills that it can be difficult to find the right one for the right job at the right time.

SERVICES

A carpenter may be able to act as a general contractor on small jobs. He'll get you an electrician or a plumber and coordinate the different trades. But a carpenter may be just a framer who does only rough, heavy-duty structural work, or he may be a trimmer, a cabinetmaker, or just a general handyman. It is unlikely that a carpenter will be all or even most of these things. That's the catch: which kind of carpenter do you hire?

I started in construction as an apprentice carpenter. It's the best way to learn how to be a general contractor. At first, an apprentice spends all day carrying lumber and nailing off plywood decking—a terrifically boring job that turns his hammering arm into a limp noodle at the end of the day. But over several years his skills develop past hauling and repetitive nailing to rough concrete formwork, layouts, framing and sheathing, then on to finishing skills like hanging doors, laying floors, and trimming. An apprentice can absorb all the specialty trades of carpentry.

I had the opportunity to build furniture, restore antiques, draw plans, and more. But most people get off this learning path as soon as they get good enough at one specialty to make a decent living. You want to find a carpenter who got off at the right place.

This kind of specialization is also likely to conflict with your expectations when you hire a carpenter. To most people the word "carpenter" is synonymous with builder—someone who can build a deck, a picnic table, a fence, or an addition on a house. You expect someone who can handle just about any kind of construction. Lower your expectations. Think of carpentry as a very general professional description. You have to find a professional who has experience with the job at hand to get the results you want.

QUALIFICATIONS

A journeyman carpenter must complete a four-year apprenticeship consisting of 8,000 hours of on-the-job training, and about 600 hours of classroom study. It's a formidable program, generally limited to union carpenters. Many union carpenters move into industrial work like building docks and railroad trestles, or into commercial work like building concrete forms on high-rise buildings.

Some residential carpenters (the ones working on the endless condominiums and garden apartments popping up where single-family houses used to be) are union-trained as well. When mass-produced carpentry work dries up, many of those carpenters supplement their income with short-term, custom work.

But for general carpentry (not railroad trestles or elegantly veneered furniture), I'd suggest a carpenter who has recently started a small general contracting firm, or one of the top carpenters (someone like the building foreman) who works for a larger residential contracting company.

I am sympathetic to small, independent general-building contractors because this is the real proving ground for carpenters. General contracting exposes them to all the building trades and to all the stages of construction. A small contracting firm will probably not be unionized but everyone learns to pull his weight quickly because a small company doing custom work does one job at a time, and each one has to show a profit and provide future recommendations.

PROFESSIONAL PRACTICES

I've worked in northern Vermont and New Hampshire, where a surprising amount of carpentry is done on the basis of a handshake—no contract, no informal written agreement, just a verbal description of the work, a price estimate, and a handshake. But 99 out of 100 times, this is a dangerous policy. The old-timer who has always worked that way, who considers the handshake as binding as a contract, who is reliable, on time, reasonably priced, and good at his job is a rarity.

Here's what you are likely to encounter. Let's assume that the gutter along the front of your house has become clogged with leaves. In the winter, rain backs up on the roof, works under the shingles, and freezes. The gutter sags, shingles work loose, leaks develop, and the corner of your roof starts to rot. A good general carpenter will have to climb up on a ladder to get a close look at the problem—disregard anyone who gives you a diagnosis or a price from the ground. For this kind of job, the carpenter will pry up a few shingles to get a clear idea of how much damage has been done.

After an inspection of the job, the carpenter might give you a report right on the spot. Be wary if you get a price on the spot as well. Instant prices tend to be inflated, while prices figured at home (they are checked and rechecked) tend to be cheaper. Your next contact should include a written estimate. This may be a primitive document, but at a minimum, it must identify all the parties involved, describe the work, the materials to be used, the total cost, the method of payment, etc.

Remember: this document is an estimate, not a contract, not an order for work. No deposit is required. No time limit is in force. Be wary of any contractor who applies pressure to sign now or lose his services. At this stage of the job, you should be comparing estimates and recommendations, reconsidering the scope of the job and your ability to pay for it. While you reconsider and compare, the carpenter should be responsive to any questions about the estimate, but don't expect him to invest more time (like another visit to the site) on speculation.

Try to keep all your options open for as long as possible. If the price of an estimate seems reasonable by comparison, and you are satisfied with the carpenter's reputation, the last roadblock is likely to be time. Most contractors have a tendency to make optimistic projections about when they can start and finish. Naturally, when they are competing for the job, they want to present the best possible picture.

Do not eliminate the competition before nailing down specific dates with the carpenter you have selected. Here's what may happen if you do. To get the job, the carpenter estimates that he can start on the first of the month. But once you give him the job the first becomes the fifth, then the tenth. The pressure is off. Now he doesn't have to adjust to your schedule. How can he do this to you? The excuses will be couched in situations you'll have a hard time objecting to. For instance, the gearbox on his truck is broken; his helper's grandmother had a heart attack, etc. An imaginative carpenter can string you along for weeks.

Avoid this common problem by getting a verbal commitment about starting and finishing dates over the phone, then in writing in the estimate before you announce your selection. One other point: take the minute required to call the carpenters you did not select; thank them for submitting their estimate. No, you don't have to, but it is unfair to turn them down by leaving them in midair after they have invested the time to come to your home and estimate the job.

EVALUATING WORK

If you don't know how to judge quality carpentry, rely on recommendations of performance. For instance, the expertise of joinery on fascia boards under the gutter, the way flashing was installed, and the way new shingles were woven into the roof may escape you, so ask the carpenter's former client the obvious question: "Does the roof still leak, or did he fix it?" You don't have to know about construction details to evaluate performance.

You can, however, spot some of the obvious signs of quality work on decks, doors, windows, trim, and other areas when looking at the contractor's past work. Look for clean carpentry that is uniform. Check for clean saw cuts, for nails that are driven without leaving hammer marks in the surrounding wood surface, for joints that are tight, and for even margins between door and frame, window and casing, baseboard and flooring.

Part of the craft of carpentry is finessing corners that don't meet at exactly 90 degrees, of fudging molding joints in corners that are out of square. But you should not be able to detect these accommodations easily. If a patch is necessary in a wood railing, it should be spliced in, sanded, and finished so it doesn't stand out.

On the business side, try to avoid carpenters who ask for a substantial amount of the job price up front. The common rationalization is that they need 20, 30, or even 40 percent of the total price in order to buy materials. Not true—almost every lumberyard will extend a line of credit to established carpenters who regularly work in the area. Many even help carpenters figure material costs for the job. There is no reason you should provide financing for the carpenter by carrying the material costs before the materials are set in place. Don't pay for lumber; pay for a deck—pay for materials as they are installed and finished, not as they arrive from the lumberyard.

GRIEVANCES

With carpenters, particularly on small, general carpentry jobs that are the most common, your agreement (whether an informal letter or a fine-print contract) is your best protection against unresolved disputes. Try to include a provision that gives you the right to apply any unpaid balance to keep the job moving if an unreasonable delay is encountered. This means if the carpenter doesn't show up for several weeks, you can hire another carpenter.

Frankly, this is a difficult provision to include in an agreement for small to moderate-size jobs—for jobs up to $1,000 or so. In these cases, the best you can do is to reserve most of the carpenter's profit (at least 15 percent of the job price) as a final payment. But I wouldn't threaten to withhold this payment lightly or frequently. The money is a matter of financial leverage to you; to the carpenter, it's food on his family's dinner table. Remember, local contractors talk to each other; if you are unreasonable with your payments, the word will get around and you may have trouble hiring local contractors in the future.

Try to work at solving disputes. The point is to get the job done. Getting mad or trying to get even will probably be counterproductive. You might say that you were asked by a neighbor to recommend a carpenter. Offering a carrot usually brings better results than applying the stick.

In many areas, a license of some kind is required for all home-repair and improvement contractors. Serious malpractice like fraudulent billing or substituting inferior, unsound materials should be brought to the attention of local licensing agencies. The possible suspension of a contractor's license constitutes extreme leverage.

The most common grievance is over quality—you thought his work would look and perform better than it does. There's not much you can do about these complaints. They are judgment calls. If the work is shabby, have the carpenter make corrections before the job is completed, while you are still in a position to do some serious bargaining. You can and should dispute specifications. If the agreement calls for Thermopane and the carpenter installed windows of single-thickness glass, you've got a case and you should pursue it.

Don't wait until the job is done to be disappointed. If you're not going to be satisfied with the work, come to grips with the problem when the work is still in progress and there's still something you can do about it. The quality of work should be monitored from day one.

Electricians

At the turn of the century, the following sign was placed on the walls of many hotel rooms:

This Room is Equipped with
EDISON ELECTRIC LIGHT
———————————
Do not attempt to light with
match. Simply turn key
on wall by the door.
The use of Electricity for lighting is in no
way harmful to health, nor does it affect
the soundness of sleep.

The final sentence ran in small print at the bottom of the sign. Yes, for a while there were a lot of people who tried to light electric bulbs like a candle. And there were doomsayers who predicted all kinds of dangerous and evil consequences from exposure to electricity.

Today, long after TVA and Rural Electrification Administration (REA), electricity does almost any job that can be done manually. A typical American home today has sixteen electrical appliances slaving away.

But underneath the convenience of microwave ovens, TVs, and ¼ in. power drills, there is still a fear of electricity. Working on home wiring is the job do-it-yourselfers are least likely to tackle. Some people won't even replace fuses. That's paranoia. But some fear is healthy. You can be killed by less electricity than it takes to light a 10-watt bulb.

SERVICES

Most apprentice programs make a distinction between outside wiremen, who work on high-tension power lines, and inside wiremen, who are trained to handle residential, commercial, and industrial work.

You can hire an independent journeyman electrician who runs his own work (he might have a few helpers), or go to a residential electrical contractor who employs a crew of journeymen electricians.

In either case, the electrician should be able to read blueprints and evaluate the electrical specifications that accompany them. If the electrician is working as a subcontractor to your general-building contractor, this information takes the form of instructions provided by an architect or engineer who drew up the plans.

But in residential construction, there is a big difference in the information supplied to the mechanical trades (electricians, plumbers, and heating contractors), and to the building trades (masons, carpenters, and general contractors). For example, house plans show details of framing, where joists and girders should be placed, what size they should be, how they should be attached to each other, and more. But the location of outlets may not be penciled in, overhead lamps and switch locations may be represented by dotted lines, not the detail drawings reserved for structural work. Wiring size, the design and layout of circuits, and other particulars are commonly left to the electrician. He has a lot of autonomy, although he must comply with the National Electrical Code and any local codes that supersede it.

A good electrician has to know how houses are put together in order to fish wiring through studs and joists without ripping apart your walls. He should be able to install the wiring required for major appliances, door bells, and underwater lights in a pool—in short, a journeyman residential electrician can wire new homes, add circuits, make repairs, and modernize older electrical systems.

QUALIFICATIONS

The International Brotherhood of Electrical Workers' (IBEW) apprentice program covers four and occasionally five years of on-the-job training supported by classroom study. It's one of the longest for construction trades. The training program is registered with the U.S. Department of Labor (USDL, Bureau of Apprenticeships and Training, 601 D St. NW, Rm. 5000, Washington, DC 20213). You can write them to find out if the contractor you're dealing with (union or not) participates in approved training programs. Contact the nearest IBEW local to find out about the thoroughness of training in your area. On completion, apprentices become journeymen electricians.

Journeymen affiliated with the National Electrical Contractors Association (NECA, 7315 Wisconsin Ave., Washington, DC 20014), subscribe to the detailed NECA Standard of Installation (make this part of your contract), offer warranties, and are trained to provide expertise in estimating, purchasing, engineering, and supervising journeymen electricians. Write them, or a local chapter, for a copy of the Standard.

But isn't the question of qualifications as simple as asking an electrician for his license? No. First, not all electricians are licensed; second, I talked to the director of training for a major IBEW local who allowed that in some out-of-the-way areas, a license to wire houses has all the authority of a license to catch fish. Granted, this is the exception, not the rule.

To find out if a license is needed where you live, contact an IBEW local, the town building department, or local consumer-protection agencies. An IBEW training or apprentice officer is in a good position to tell you if the license indicates real expertise.

PROFESSIONAL PRACTICES

I don't want to give you step-by-step accounts of common electrical installations because, while I will encourage you to try all kinds of do-it-yourself jobs, I suggest you call in a qualified electrician instead of experimenting if you have the slightest doubt about even the most basic electrical projects.

Strict adherence to electrical codes is the most important standard of practice. All contracts should contain a phrase like this: "All materials must be UL listed, and all work and materials must conform strictly to the National Electrical Code, and to all local codes." Underwriter's Laboratories (UL, 207 E. Ohio St., Chicago, IL 60611) is the testing laboratory that sets many product standards in the industry and determines if manufacturers have met these standards before a UL listing is granted. For more details on contracts (or a copy of the National Code for $8.25) write the International Association of Electrical Inspectors (IAEI, 802 Busse Hwy., Park Ridge, IL 60668).

Just as electrician's licensing is not standardized or absolute, neither is residential electrical inspection. Many new homeowners believe that in addition to framing inspections by the building department, a separate electrical inspection has to be made before a certificate is granted. It's called the Certificate of Acceptance, granted by the Board of Fire Underwriters, and unless you get it, you can't get a Certificate of Occupancy (C.O.). Without the C.O., you can't legally live there.

All this is true in New York State. It's not true anywhere else. The New York Board of Fire Underwriters (NYBFU, 85 John St., New York, NY 10038) is the only independent, nonprofit inspection board left. If you live in New York, and the work of your electrician is approved by this board, you got quality work. In metropolitan areas outside New York, a separate electrical inspection is likely to be made by a building inspector specifically qualified to evaluate electrical work. As you get farther away from cities, building departments become less specialized; one inspector may check the framing, plumbing, wiring—the works. This starts to be marginal electrical safety protection.

However, this kind of inspection is still better than the two other possibilities. One is called self-certification, *i.e.,* the electrician inspects his own work. (Don't you wonder how many give themselves violations?) The other, worse yet, is the current practice in New Jersey and a few other states. You hire one of several private, profit-making electrical-inspection firms to get their certificate, and then your C.O. Some of these firms let their inspectors work on a commission basis. Does that inspire confidence? Electrical-safety inspection managed like a used-car lot?

Find out where you stand. Call the building department, local consumer-protection agencies, and your home insurance agent— without an inspection, without a C.O., you will not even get adequate insurance coverage on your home.

EVALUATING WORK

A NECA profile of their typical electrical contractor provides these facts: he is forty-five years old, a high school graduate with some college, has worked as a journeyman electrician for five years before starting his own contracting company (that's in addition to at least four years of apprenticeship, or nine years of training), and has $30,000 invested in trucks, tools, and equipment.

A brand-new company (check age of business with the Better Business Bureau) may mean you're dealing with a brand-new journeyman electrician. Ask for recommendations (and check the reputations of all electricians who estimate your job) from local general building contractors, architects, the building department, and IBEW local. Also ask each electrician if a license is required where you live, and if he has one. Then ask if a Certificate of Acceptance or some other inspection is necessary, and how it will be conducted. Verify his answers at the building department.

One small point. If your home has the standard, glass-faced fuses (modern systems use circuit breakers instead), you can evaluate the electrician's diagnosis of some problems by checking the fuse window. An overload (drawing excessive current) melts the thin metal strip across the face of the fuse. Unloading the circuit, *i.e.,* distributing electrical appliances and lamps to draw roughly equal amounts of current from each circuit, may solve this problem. If this is impractical, ask the electrician about adding a new circuit. However, a short-circuit (the kind of problem you need an electrician to solve) vaporizes the metal strip, which discolors the fuse window.

GRIEVANCES

Take unreconcilable complaints to your IBEW local for union electricians, NECA for affiliated contractors, the building department for technical or installation problems, consumer-protection agencies and the Better Business Bureau for improper business practices.

Substandard, unapproved work and materials should be caught by the inspector who approves building plans before a permit is issued, or the inspector who checks the work. But if you want further safeguards, ask for details on equipment and procedures from the Consumer Product Safety Commission (CPSC, 7315 Wisconsin Ave. NW, Washington, DC 20207; 800-658-8326, or 800-492-2937 in Maryland).

I suggest you write the CPSC if you have aluminum wiring (stamped AL every few feet on the wire sheath). If your home was built between 1965 and 1973, it's very possible you do. The CPSC can give you the gory details of aluminum wiring; they estimate that within a ten-year period over five hundred fires can be directly attributed to problems with aluminum wiring. The connections made between aluminum conductors and copper terminals on switches and receptacles is one problem; oxidization of exposed aluminum wires is another. Ask your electrician about a solution called pigtailing.

Exterminators

Every two out of five homes have some degree of termite infestation. In some areas, the problem is so severe that termite inspections are required by banks before they will give you a mortgage. But termites are only one of the more than eight thousand species of insects causing property damage in North America.

According to the National Pest Control Association, the ten most common household pests are cockroaches, mice, rats, termites, ants and carpenter ants, fleas, ticks, spiders, and silverfish. Control of these pests is a surprisingly complex matter that is usually beyond the capabilities of widely advertised, over-the-counter remedies. Successful treatment can be difficult for three reasons: first, the tremendous variation of pest species (the United States has fifty-five varieties of cockroaches, including one that produces forty offspring every thirty days); second, environmental variation like differences in food sources, weather conditions, and home construction across the country; and third, the plethora of pesticides, some thirty thousand of them, including those used in agriculture, that may do damage to specific pests and other living matter—including you.

SERVICES

Pest control is one area of home care that is highly susceptible to fly-by-night practices, particularly in cities. Here's how a typical scam operates. It starts with a bang as you are offered or "win" a free inspection. This news is announced by someone in a clean uniform of the mythical pest control outfit, or even from someone posing as an inspector from the Department of Health. After a quick look in a few kitchen cabinets, the fly-by-nighter produces a vial of cockroaches, alive and kicking. He says they came from your kitchen cupboards. They didn't—they came from his truck where he takes very good care of them. To solve the problem, a price per gallon for XYZ Cockroach Chemical is agreed on, and thirty minutes later you discover that your home has soaked up barrels of the stuff.

Reputable professional exterminators, on the other hand, should be able to inspect your home thoroughly, identify pests and the degree of infestation, locate entry points and nesting areas, and recommend safe, effective treatments. Only pesticides registered with the Environmental Protection Agency should be used. Somewhere on the label you should see EPA Reg. No. and several digits.

QUALIFICATIONS

All states require certification of pest control operators, or PCOs as the professionals prefer to be called. However, technicians in the field are not required to be certified as long as they work under the supervision of a certified PCO. But the PCO may be back at the office doing paperwork. If you pay for expert service, make sure you deal with the expert.

Incidentally, this is one of the few hands-on home care and repair fields where women professionals are not uncommon. Apparently, many companies have found that women technicians and PCOs are more readily accepted into a home than their male counterparts. But male or female, certification is essential, even though standards vary from state to state. For example, Virginia requires certification for all PCOs while neighboring Maryland requires PCO certification for individuals *and* licensing for pest control companies. All state programs must equal or exceed minimim EPA guidelines.

The National Pest Control Association (NPCA) requires applicants to have at least one year of professional experience, and to subscribe to their code of ethics and bylaws. All their members must be certified. Membership in the NPCA or an autonomous state pest control association is a good indicator of sound business practice and technical expertise.

PROFESSIONAL PRACTICES

Pest control operators should conduct a thorough investigation of your home, concentrating on the kitchen, bathroom, any dark or damp areas, and entry points where walls join floors and ceilings, and where house foundations meet the ground. The inspection should be more than skin deep in order to locate nesting areas, for example, in the depths of undersink cabinets that have never seen the light of day.

Warranties vary widely according to the species of pests, conditions of construction, pesticides used, and the company doing the work. There are no standards. The National Pest Control Association estimates that termite control warranties have now been reduced to an average of one year, sometimes with extensions (a form of service contract), available for a fee. Cockroach treatment may be warrantied for only six months or not at all. Each company is different, but look twice at outlandish promises of long-term protection.

Would you deal with a company you knew absolutely nothing about? That's what a lot of apartment dwellers do when their landlord posts a list in the lobby to sign up for the exterminator. The list is public, but the exterminator is not. He's the landlord's exterminator, or brother—who knows? Ask. If you don't get good answers, if you can't get in touch with the exterminator, find your own. You are allowed to have visitors, whether they are friends or home care professionals, without the landlord's permission.

If you contact several exterminators, expect the estimates to vary considerably. The Washington-based Health Research Group recently conducted a study of Washington area pest control firms, and found virtually no relationship between price and quality of service. (Now isn't that reassuring?) For example, similar cockroach treatments in a six-room apartment ranged from $12.50 to $57.50. This should tell you not to select one of several PCOs by price alone unless you are positive that all are offering similar treatments, warranties, and expertise.

Pest control firms are in competition with each other, and with nature. A new twist in natural extermination is being sold by mail-order firms. Some legitimate companies sell things like ladybugs that eat about two and a half times their weight in mealy bugs, moth eggs, spider mites, and other creatures every day. However, only some of these beneficial insects may arrive able to eat anything. Some shady mail-order firms have a costly sense of humor. The Better Business Bureau has documented cases where a "Foolproof Natural Method for Killing Pests" turns out to be two wood blocks with instructions to put the pest on one block and hit it with the other. Couldn't be more natural, right? You wouldn't catch them selling plastic blocks.

Any chemical treatment is serious business. It must be done carefully, according to label directions, and not in combination with other agents; dishes or food must be out of the way, and, most important, so must people who are not wearing protective clothing. The EPA, which regulates all pesticides, maintains a list of suspended and canceled pesticides. Some substances like Kepone and Lindane have been banned, while others are only restricted. Dieldin and Aldin, for example, are limited to below-ground use. Most Chlordane products (a very common termite treatment) were banned by 1981 except for below-ground application. Unfortunately, in many areas you can still buy varying concentrations of this chemical over the counter. Write the EPA (Office of Pesticide Programs, Washington, DC 20460) for their restricted list. It is constantly under review as new test results are analyzed.

EVALUATING WORK

Check the contractor's reputation, particularly the long-term effectiveness of his treatments, with former clients. Ask the PCO specifically what methods of treatment and chemical agents will be used. You can verify these procedures with the NPCA and local pest control organizations. Check recommended chemicals with the EPA (be very wary about pesticides on their restricted list), and both state and local health departments. Some states, notably California, have regulations significantly stiffer than the minimum EPA standards.

Another excellent source of recommendations and information on approved methods of treating all types of pests is your local U.S. Department of Agriculture county agent. Look in your phone book. Every county has one. You can inquire about the firm's business reputation at the local Better Business Bureau.

GRIEVANCES

Complaints about PCOs should be directed to local trade associations and the National Pest Control Association (NPCA, 8150 Leesburg Pike, Vienna, VA 22180), which maintains a grievance committee.

In addition, you can refer fraudulent or dangerous practices to state certification boards. If the pest control company is licensed (true only in some states), you can apply pressure on the company as well as the operator.

Floor-covering Contractors

The floors of most new homes are framed with wood timbers called joists, then covered with sheets of plywood to make a subfloor. This is strong enough to walk on and to support your furniture. The trouble is that the subfloor looks just like what it is—rough, grainy, knot-filled plywood. It can be covered with materials selected for strength, resilience, insulation value, or maintenance-free service.

A lot of floor coverings, particularly resilient floor tile and some varieties of carpeting, are installed by do-it-yourselfers and do not require a lot of specialized, expensive tools, or technical expertise. Of course, if you want a tile bathroom with curving vanities and sunken tubs, you'd be wise to hire a professional. But with a lot of floor covering work, the quality of the subfloor and the material you put down are even more important than the contractor's expertise.

Not all floor-covering work is done by independent, self-employed, home contractors—some is done by an installer who works for the department store, the floor-covering emporium, or the carpet warehouse where you made your purchase. In these cases, a salesman sells you the product first, and the installation services second, almost as an afterthought. This presents a problem: you can't hire and fire the installer the way you would an independent contractor. Your grievances must be handled differently, as I'll explain later.

SERVICES

On new construction, finished wood flooring, tile, or carpeting should be one of the last materials installed or else the new finish will become old overnight as electricians, plumbers, and carpenters traipse in and out. The general contractor (G.C.) should see to this. Part of his job is making sure that everyone shows up at the right time with the right materials, and that no professional toes (or egos) are stepped on. Hold the general contractor responsible for the finished job.

For work in existing homes (called old work as opposed to jobs under construction), you can hire an independent contractor or go through a store where you buy the material. If you end up with a flooring-store installer, the store becomes a kind of general contrac-

51

tor and you must make them responsible for the work.

It is difficult for independent contractors to give you the shopping services available in a store where aisle after aisle of different styles and varieties are displayed. But don't buy from a store that treats installation as an afterthought. Make sure these services are detailed before you sign a contract or a check.

An independent flooring contractor will make a trip to your home to inspect the existing floor; he will see if it can be covered or if it must be removed and repaired first. He will check if your subfloor is flat enough and strong enough to carry the new material; if the floor is square and true, or irregular; and if there are obstructions like heat registers and radiator pipes. Then he will give you an estimate.

Beware of flat installation rates ("prefinished oak parquet, $6.10 per sq. ft. installed") given before the installer or the salesman has seen the job. That advertised figure may grow if their version of a flooring installation applies only to ideal conditions. Few homes have true, flat, sound floors, even when they're new.

QUALIFICATIONS

Judge a flooring contractor's qualifications on the basis of recommendations first, and then by how accurately he presents the specifications, advantages, and disadvantages of floor-covering options.

Don't get weak in the knees when a contractor who works with one or two kinds of flooring gives them fabulous recommendations. What else is he going to do? A contractor in your home or a salesman in the store should be able to give you accurate thumbnail sketches of many different materials; he should discuss covering size, finish, durability, maintenance requirements, price, and cost of installation.

Here are a few representative costs for standard floor coverings. The prices for materials and labor are averages from *The 1981 National Construction Estimator 29th Edition* (Craftsman Book Co.; 542 Stevens Ave., Solana Beach, CA 92075; $10.75), a book contractors use to help them figure estimates.

Hardwood oak strip flooring: a moderately priced, easily installed, durable floor if sealed and coated with wax or polyurethane; available in many grades; 25/32 in. x 2¼ in. graded Standard and Better; $2.45/sq. ft. for materials, 74 cents/sq. ft. for labor.

Oak parquet: moderately priced, 12 x 12 in., 5/16 in. thick, prefinished, needs a solid subfloor; installed with adhesive; about the same cost as oak strip flooring; *clear acrylic impregnated parquet squares*, also prefinished but more durable, are rated at $5/sq. ft., and $1.20 for labor.

Vinyl asbestos tile: 1/16 in. thick will show most imperfections in the subfloor; 38 cents/sq. ft. for material, 29 cents for labor; thicker 1/8 in. tile is 64 cents for material.

Vinyl sheet flooring: very careful measuring is the secret; .065 in. thick is 55 cents/sq. ft., 40 cents for labor; thicker, more resilient sheeting (.090 in.) with a vinyl-wearing layer is more durable and nearly maintenance-free; $1.05/sq. ft. for material, 40 cents for labor.

Quarry tile: a very durable tile good for entry ways and kitchens; 6 in. unglazed squares are $1.60/sq. ft. for material, $3.16 for labor; the best quality installation is called a mud set (tiles are set in cement); thin set using adhesive is less durable; 6 in. glazed tiles are listed at $4.34/sq. ft. for material, $5.09 for labor.

Ceramic tile: endless styles, shapes, and finishes are available; 4 x 4 in. glazed tile set in cement mortar is rated at $2.54/sq. ft. for material, $3.51 for labor; used with rounded tiles called a sanitary cove, and wall tile for highly sanitary installations in baths.

Marble: for your villa figure a mere $8/sq. ft. for 7/8 in. thick marble flooring and $4.70/sq. ft. for the installation; a 12 x 12 ft. entry hall will cost you only a little over $1,800.

Acrylic carpeting: 40 oz. weight over a 50 oz. pad is rated at $12.50/sq. yd. and $3.45 for labor; acrylics look like wool, wear like nylon, resist sun fading, and clean easily; flame-retardant should be included.

Continuous filament nylon carpeting: 24 oz. weight over a 50 oz. pad is rated at $7.50/sq. yd. for material, $3.45 for labor; nylon is less resilient than wool but not as easily damaged by abrasion; water-soluble stains are easy to clean; check anti-static features.

Antron nylon carpeting: 21 oz. weight of anti-static carpet is listed at $11.60/sq. yd. for material, $3.45 for labor.

Commercial wool carpeting: over a 50 oz. pad, rated at $20.04/sq. yd. for material, $3.45 for labor; easy to clean, very durable and resilient.

Remember the other criteria for selecting either a contractor or a retailer. Ask for three names of former clients who have had work done that is similar to the job you have planned. Better yet, follow a firsthand recommendation from a friend where you can inspect the work yourself, ask about price, durability, and if the contractor or flooring dealer fulfilled his commitments.

PROFESSIONAL PRACTICES

After inspecting the job site, a contractor should make recommendations of coverings that will provide the appearance and service you require. Feel free to ask for estimates using two or three grades of flooring, which will show, for example, how the different materials affect the over-all job price.

A floor-covering contractor should provide a contract including dimensions of the work area, materials and installation work required to prepare the subfloor, and the manufacturer, catalogue number, size, color, finish, and amount of flooring material needed. The method of installation should be stipulated and, if required, surface finishing should be also. The price should list materials and labor separately.

If the floor-covering job has to be synchronized with a larger home-improvement project, be definite about delivery and installation dates. If the carpet arrives before the plywood subflooring, you'll have a storage problem. If the carpeting arrives a week after the contractor is ready to start, you'll probably lose him.

A knowledgeable contractor or dealer will ask specific questions about your floor. For example, what kind of use does it get? Is it a pass-through from one part of the home to another? Does the floor get a lot of direct sunlight? If a dealer doesn't have his installer or salesman come to your home for a look, call a dealer who will. If ads for the flooring you want, at a price you like, don't pan out because the store just ran out, beware. You may be getting suckered into a bait and switch routine. It's illegal to lure customers into a store with empty ads and promises. Report these dealers to local consumer-protection agencies and the Better Business Bureau. Shop somewhere else.

EVALUATING WORK

Your best bet is to check work done by the contractor or dealer in person. For carpeting, installers should use knee kickers (tools that grab the carpet at one end while the installer applies force at the other) to stretch the material flat before attaching it to tackless strips around the border of the area. These are thin strips of plywood with staggered nailheads protruding up to sink into the carpet. If joints are required, they should be sewn. Don't accept installation procedures that use double-faced tape; that's a cheap, do-it-yourself version.

For wood flooring look for a flat surface, closed seams, a uniform finish, and accurate, even margins around obstructions like pipes that rise through the floor to feed baseboard radiators. Look at the details on stair nosings, treads, and risers. The evidence of surface nailing (small holes filled with putty to match the wood finish) should be barely noticeable.

For vinyl tile the quality of the subfloor is crucial. You won't see it beneath the tile, but if the job wasn't done right you will see all the problems of the subfloor mirrored in the floor covering. Look for tight, even joints, and an equal margin of partial tiles at the edges of the room, a sign of a careful layout.

For ceramic and quarry tile look for even seams tightly filled with grout. Cracked grout is evidence of a poorly prepared subfloor. For extra durability, some contractors will coat the grout with a layer of liquid silicone, particularly in baths, to keep water out and minimize deterioration.

GRIEVANCES

In an unregulated trade like this, you should make every effort to resolve disputes while the job is in progress, before final payment is made. With independent contractors, rely on the protections built into your contract. With installers who work for a store, involve the salesman at the first sign of trouble. Don't let the people who sold you the product disappear while the installer takes all the heat.

If your complaints involve product quality or durability, you should involve the manufacturer as well. This is one good reason for buying well-known, long-established national brands. Major companies have the resources to provide consumers services. Olin, for example, has an informative guide called ''The Carpet Report'' (write Olin at 120 Long Ridge Rd., Stamford, CT 06904).

You can also contact the Carpet and Rug Institute (CRI, Director of Consumer Affairs, 1629 K St. NW, Suite 700, Washington, DC

20006). They had an active consumer-complaint department, and although they no longer follow up on cases, they can help with general consumer information.

If problems arise over money, or failure to honor the business provisions of a contract, and the leverage of holding the final payment doesn't get results, go to local consumer-protection agencies and follow grievance guidelines in the Primer.

General Building Contractors

A recent study by the Federal Trade Commission and the Department of Housing and Urban Development found that anyone buying a newly built home will, on average, find defects that cost $1,000 to repair. The study also found that two-thirds of the new homes had at least one construction problem that the builder did not fix. And the average cost of repairs in these homes was over $1,400.

One in five new homeowners in the study had a serious disagreement with their builder, one in fifteen consulted an attorney, and one in twenty-five hired one. The complaints varied—interior problems with floors, walls, and ceilings were on top of the list, then problems with yard drainage and exterior masonry. These were followed by roofing and plumbing problems. And by way of demolishing the tired adage "you get what you pay for," the number of construction problems increased in new homes priced over $80,000. (And they also increased those under $30,000.)

I'm telling you this not to kill your enthusiasm about buying or building a new home, to add on or make major alterations to the place where you live, but to underscore the importance of hiring a reliable, experienced, professional contractor. Few people are well qualified to be general contractors. They have an enormous job. Imagine what it's like coordinating all the elements of construction; dealing with architects, masons, plumbers, electricians, roofers, and clients (that's you). General contractors start six mornings a week at the lumberyard, picking up windows or hardware; they put in a day's labor on the job, going over detail after option after color after price with the owner. They check in with the building inspector and the bank—it's a long and busy day.

If the general contractor can put all these pieces together, a poorly planned, boring, bargain-basement project can wind up looking and working like a swiss watch. But if the G.C. is missing even a few pieces of the puzzle, your award-winning blueprints and million-dollar materials will be transformed into a test house for do-it-yourself repair projects that eat up your budget and your weekends.

SERVICES

A good general contractor is to construction what a good general practitioner is to medicine. You wouldn't call in a G.C. for limited, technical jobs like converting your furnace from oil to gas, or adding a new electrical circuit. But you would be wise to follow the G.C.'s recommendation of a heating contractor or an electrician, just the way you would trust your family G.P. to recommend a surgeon.

The G.C. looks at your home the way a G.P. looks at your health—as a whole. A G.C. keeps track of all the little details the way a G.P. keeps your medical history. He has to plan and price every component in an estimate; he looks over everyone's shoulder once the job begins. The G.C. has to make sure you're getting the right concrete mix ratio even though part of the money you're paying him is going for the services of a mason subcontractor.

The G.C. builds bridges over the gaps where one trade stops and another starts. He may not know as much about concrete as the mason, as much about septic systems as the plumber, or as much about wiring as the electrician, but a good G.C. knows enough about each one to make sure that the mason leaves the right-size opening for the soil pipe, and doesn't leave it in the best location for a fuse box.

A good G.C. has to manage money and contracts. He has to communicate with mortgage bankers and loan officers in the morning and concrete laborers in the afternoon. He has to read blueprints and personalities. You think a family G.P. has to hold your hand? Wait till the excavation on your dream addition fills with water from a week's worth of rain.

Don't underestimate the value of a G.C. who can deal effectively with people. Before I made the jump from carpenter to general contractor, I worked for a G.C. who aged visibly on a job where the electrician chopped holes in the heating contractor's return plenum because it blocked the only path between his Bx cables and the fuse box. That's a nice surprise package at 8:00 A.M. Friday morning when the electrician has decided to leave early for a weekend hunting trip. This kind of confrontation, though not always so extreme, happens all the time.

Most G.C.s are former carpenters. Many do all their own woodwork. Some use only two subcontractors (a heating contractor and an electrician) and do everything else themselves. Regardless of what the general contractor does or doesn't do himself, you'll be paying for complete building services and supervision, from layout and excavation to trimming and painting.

On top of all this, a good G.C. has to give you something else—confidence. If he can give you every service I've described except this one, don't hire him. When confidence in a contractor's expertise or honesty erodes, the relationship gets ugly.

QUALIFICATIONS

After reading the section on services, it should be clear that it takes many years for a general contractor to get enough over-all building experience to do a really good job. I wouldn't hire a G.C. who's had less than five years of building experience (consider that a bare minimum) without exceptional firsthand professional recommendations.

You can get a lot of help finding a G.C. On large projects where an architect is involved, part of his job is to recommend contractors, and help evaluate their bids. Without an architect, ask for recommendations from friends and neighbors of course, also from housing and real-estate experts who deal with local G.C.s all the time: mortgage bankers and loan officers, building inspectors, realtors, appraisers, town tax assessors, home insurance agents, and real-estate attorneys for a start.

This should get you a list of names. Eliminate potential bad apples by concentrating on business qualifications first. Check the local Better Business Bureau, and consumer-protection agencies. This is important when you deal with remodeling contractors, and critical when the contractor sells a specialized or proprietary product like "custom-sculptured masonry siding."

Next, write the Federal Housing Administration (FHA, HUD

Printing Office, 451 7th St. SW, Washington, DC 20410) for a copy of their DSI list. It carries the names of roughly 1,500 general builders who are Debarred, Suspended, and Ineligible Contractors. Most build multi-family housing like condominiums, though some build single-family homes as well. Contractors make the DSI list for price gouging, fraud, deceptive advertising, and cute tricks like jiggling the cement content in concrete to save a little money. Check with a loan officer at your bank. He'll probably have the current list, which is updated monthly.

From the remaining list of contractors who come highly recommended, I'd give special consideration to those who offer warranty programs. (If you want a detailed look at what you may be in for as a homeowner, write the Superintendent of Documents, U.S. Government Printing Office, Washington, DC 20402, for a copy of the statistical but fascinating report, "A Survey of Homeowner Experience with Residential Housing Construction.") On new homes, investigate the Home Owner's Warranty Program (HOW) run by the largest, most active group in the field, the National Association of Home Builders. It's like a giant service contract covering structural defects, mechanical systems, and more. Write HOW (National Housing Center, 15th and M Sts. NW, Washington, DC 20005) for details. A one-time homeowner deductible of $250 was added in 1981, along with a surcharge paid by builders with excessive claims. HOW officials report that fewer than twenty-five of the sixteen thousand builders in the program fall into the excessive complaint and claim category.

On existing homes, the National Association of Realtors (NAR, 430 N. Michigan Ave., Chicago, IL 60511) has approved a limited number of companies offering warranties. Write them for the list. This program is not available everywhere. It includes a home inspection to warranty structural soundness, mechanical systems, roofing, and other components at the time of sale. Cost is roughly one-half of 1 percent of the sale price, or $200 on a $40,000 home.

PROFESSIONAL PRACTICES

For the uninitiated, start your dealings with a G.C. by writing HUD for a copy of their "Homeowner's Glossary of Building Terms" (HUD Publication Service Center, Room B258, 451 7th St.

SW, Washington, DC 20410). When you cut your recommended list to three or four names and ask them for estimates, at least you'll know what they're talking about.

Make sure that all the contractors bid on the same set of plans. If contractors have a special alternative for you, ask them to price it separately. Give them time to do some careful figuring and cut the fat out of their price. When I was busy on a job during the day, it took me a week of evenings to estimate a new house from a set of blueprints and specifications.

If you have faith in your own research, and confidence in the few remaining names, you should take the lowest bid, and go to contract. Use contract forms approved by the American Institute of Architects (AIA, 1735 New York Ave. NW, Washington, DC 20006), and check the financial provisions with your bank (you'll have to if you're getting a loan for the project) and an attorney. Ask all your questions, and bring out all the gremlins before you sign.

A building contractor should keep you informed of job progress and warn you, for example, about lumber deliveries and other details. On new home construction, of course, the G.C. takes care of all this himself. On major additions and alterations, do everything you can to help, but don't sign yourself up in a Saturday morning apprentice program. Let the professional do the work. You can make the coffee.

Sit down once a week with your G.C. to review the progress of the job, potential problems, and upcoming payments. Toward the end of a big project you and your contractor will start counting the money very carefully (you will be counting what you still have to pay, he will be looking at his profit). You'll also start asking for corrections and finishing touches. But the contractor may not be prepared to oblige.

The list of finishing touches and corrections is called the checklist—it drives G.C.s crazy. Include every detail, every little job that would make the project perfect. You'll never get all of them done, but it puts you in a good bargaining position. The G.C. may respond to most of the entries on your list with three nasty initials, N.I.C.— Not In Contract, which translates: you want it, you pay extra for it.

If you're working with an architect, you have a built-in mediator. If not, you have to be realistic: give up one demand to get another; barter. Your only other recourse is to include a provision in the contract for outside mediation. But try not to let things get that out of hand.

EVALUATING WORK

Building contractors provide so many services that you should evaluate them trade by trade using the entries for masons, carpenters, roofers, and others. Although the contractor may not do all this work himself, you should evaluate the joints on hardwood flooring, the operation of windows and doors, and the amount of dampness in the basement as though the builder did everything himself. He's responsible for the quality of work done by all the subcontractors.

If you want to check on construction details and procedures the builder uses, try one of the following books: for new homes, *Wood-Frame House Construction* (Handbook No. 73—it's recently revised—USDA Forest Service, U.S. Government Printing Office, Washington, DC 20402; cat. no. 0-572-135); for existing homes, *New Life for Old Dwellings* (Handbook No. 481, USDA Forest Service, U.S. Government Printing Office, Washington, DC 20402; cat. no. 1979-300-038). Both books are extensive and detailed.

If you want to verify the types of building materials the builder is using (sizes and grades should be detailed in the specifications), write the National Forest Products Association, 1619 Massachusetts Ave. NW, Washington, DC 20036. They have consumer and technical literature ranging from tables of lumber grades and wood species to pamphlets on building fire safety into new construction.

For specialty-building contractors who provide limited services or use proprietary materials or construction techniques, you can evaluate their practices, from advertising and promotional selling to contract writing and job performance, by writing the Better Business Bureau (BBB, 1150 17th St. NW, Washington, DC 20036) for publication number 311-25131, ''Standards of Practice for the Home Improvement Industry.''

But the traits that are most difficult to evaluate are probably the most important. How can you be sure the contractor is honest and completely reliable? You can't. You can get endless recommendations, but you have to trust your own instincts.

GRIEVANCES

In most areas, building contractors are licensed. In addition to standard grievance procedures outlined in the Primer, you should take serious, unreconciled complaints to the licensing agency. It is usually the local consumer-protection agency.

For affiliated builders, contact the Director of Consumer Affairs, National Association of Home Builders (NAHB, 15th and M Sts. NW, Washington, DC 20005). Problems with the HOW program should be directed to the NAHB at the same address.

If the dispute centers on materials rather than methods, involve the manufacturer. And don't forget your building inspector. His job is to make sure that all materials and methods of construction used on the job conform to local building codes. If your builder doesn't get the proper permits, if he doesn't call for a framing inspection, if a Certificate of Acceptance is not issued covering all electrical work, the inspector can legally require your builder to open up the walls, replace materials that are not code-approved, and rebuild construction that does not follow the blueprints on which the building permit was issued. This is all done at the builder's expense, and sometimes the inspector will tack on cash penalties as well. Make sure your contract contains a provision stating that all work done by the builder and all subcontractors must be code-approved.

Heating Contractors

Everybody is on the bandwagon: turn down the thermostat, convert from oil to gas, install a flue damper, buy an airtight stove, wear a sweater, save 10 percent, 20 percent, 50 percent. Fuel-saving is patriotic—nobody's against it, but it has developed almost a carnival atmosphere, complete with front men huckstering incredible claims.

I recently assembled a stack of fuel-saving literature detailing about thirty different ways to upgrade a furnace, to insulate, to weatherstrip, etc. Each project made an energy-saving claim—a 5 percent saving for wrapping the heat ducts, 10 percent for something else. I added up the offered savings, and found that I could cut my annual heating fuel costs by 120 percent. Not bad. Also, not true.

In 1978 the Department of Energy's Monthly Energy Report showed that natural gas was about 15 cents cheaper than fuel oil for the same amount of heat. In 1979 reports, gas was 36 cents cheaper. That's the year oil prices went up 50 percent. For a family in Washington, D.C., this jump was equivalent to moving their home to Minnesota. And for families in Minnesota it was plain ridiculous.

The United States has about 6 percent of the world's population, but we use about 35 percent of its energy. The business of importing oil has political strings attached to it. Electricity produced by nuclear power was the wave of the future when commercial operation began in 1957—it has some risky strings attached. Solar is now the wave of the future, but it's still in the future.

In the meantime, you've got to figure out whether you should convert from oil to gas, buy a high-efficiency, flame-retention burner, a clock thermostat, or a flue damper. You want to find a contractor who has kept up with the explosion of fuel-saving, heating-efficiency information—a contractor who can get the most out of the heating system you have, and tell you when it makes sense to upgrade it or replace it.

The wave of the future may be nuclear, solar, geothermal, or synthetic fuel, but right now you have to get through the next winter.

SERVICES

Point number one: try to make all of your decisions about conversion, replacement, new installation, and servicing in the summer. This will give you time to consider your options more carefully, and will probably save you some money since more contractors will be looking for work.

A heating contractor should be able to provide a wide range of services: calculate heat loads (figure how many BTUs you need to stay warm); match these requirements to heating equipment; install, tune, service, and make emergency repairs on your heating system. It's smart to deal with one contractor who can handle everything. If one professional figures the heating load, another sells the furnace, another installs it, another services it, and another comes in for emergencies, each one of them can lay responsibility for problems on the other guy.

Factory-authorized dealers and contractors (check with the manufacturer to make sure the Yellow Pages listing isn't bogus) have a lot of technical resources behind them. But you should hear about a lot of systems and different manufacturers, including small, built-in electric heaters to complete heating systems. A good contractor should help you evaluate the different heating systems considering the availability and price of fuel where you live. There's a lot to evaluate.

Electric furnaces are clean (there is no exhaust) and require little maintenance but are an expensive energy source. Gas furnaces that heat air or water need infrequent maintenance (cleaning and tuning every third year is standard), and currently are cheap to run—at least as long as gas is controlled, and oil is decontrolled. Oil furnaces that heat air or water need annual maintenance and regular oil deliveries. Prices for equipment and installations for these three systems are roughly equal, except that with oil heat, you can add on about $400, the typical cost of installing a 275-gal. oil tank. In moderate climates, where heating and cooling demands are approximately equal, your contractor should explain the possible advantages of heat pumps (a reversible air conditioner giving heat in winter, cooling in summer).

Furnaces are manufactured in different configurations for different types of construction. In new homes, consider integrated systems like Plen-Wood, which eliminates ductwork by using the entire insulated crawl space as a giant distribution plenum. (Write Western Wood Products Association, Yeon Bldg., Portland, OR 97204 for details.)

Some heating contractors are now specializing in upgrading existing furnaces and furnace conversion because of the energy crunch. Beware of exaggerated energy-saving claims. Look closely at dealers and contractors selling and installing a one-of-a-kind flue damper or high-efficiency burner, for example. The professional should provide clear, dollars-and-cents estimates of the cost of conversion or upgrading, and, using your utility rates (not national averages that are easy to jiggle), tell you exactly how long it will take to get your investment back in reduced fuel costs. A payback under five years is good, up to seven years is marginal, and up to ten years is probably not worth the effort. For a complete, technical analysis, write the EPA (Office of Planning and Evaluation, Washington, DC 20506) for a copy of "An Analysis of the Economics of Replacing Existing Residential Furnaces and Boilers with High-Efficiency Units."

QUALIFICATIONS

To find a qualified, full service heating contractor, ask for recommendations from general building contractors, architects, bankers, and building inspectors. Contact the Mechanical Contractors Association of America (MCAA, 5530 Wisconsin Ave. NW, Suite 750,

Washington, DC 20015) and the National Association of Plumbing-Heating-Cooling Contractors (NAPHCC, 1016 20th St. NW, Washington, DC 20036).

In most areas, the contractor needs a license to operate. Check with your local consumer-protection agency or the town building department. Look for an established firm and check the age of the business and its complaint records with the Better Business Bureau; it takes many years to absorb the peculiarities of local building and plumbing codes, and to establish productive relationships with supply houses, inspectors, and general contractors.

If you have invested a lot of time selecting a G.C. for your project, follow his recommendations. On new homes or additions it is customary for the builder to hire a heating subcontractor. The G.C. will be responsible for the quality of work you get.

Evaluating the qualifications of conversion or upgrading specialists is more difficult. Try this. Listen to what the specialist has to say (particularly on installation and performance), get the details in a written estimate, then mail a copy to the product manufacturer with this list of questions:

1. Does this contractor do business with your company on a regular basis?

2. Are you satisfied with his business practices?

3. Does the installation described in the estimate conform to your recommendations?

4. Do the energy-saving claims conform to verified company findings?

5. If the estimate appears to be substandard, could you recommend another local contractor who has your confidence?

If the company doesn't bother to answer, or discloses major discrepancies, reconsider the contractor, and perhaps the product as well.

PROFESSIONAL PRACTICES

There is a piece of heating equipment and an installation method to meet any circumstance. To make the right match, a heating contractor must inspect your home thoroughly—even to install an automatic flue damper or a flue-mounted heat extractor. Some of these appliances are heat activated; others are tripped electronically. It gets complicated, and the wrong match could retard exhaust flow, lower exhaust temperature, change combustion ratios, and cause other problems.

Many contracting firms have an engineer on staff to calculate home heating loads. They'll check the total glass area, insulation, weatherstripping, and a lot more. Then these requirements are matched to appropriate heating equipment that is detailed in a written estimate. It should include specifications of the appliances (BTU output, not input, is the heat you'll get), installation, heat delivery system, controls (like a thermostat), warranties, and costs.

Before the estimate becomes a contract, be sure it contains some method of verifying performance. A common specification reads, "The heating system must be capable of heating the home to 70°F. inside when the outside temperature is 0°F." Adjust the temperatures here to fit your needs.

Expect a carefully planned installation. Thermostats should be centrally located on an interior wall subject to average inside temperatures. Baseboard radiators or hot-air registers should be placed where they can distribute heat efficiently—not behind a couch or under a bed. In kitchens, narrow registers should be installed in the toe space between floors and cabinets.

Ask about zoned heat delivery. For example, if the bedrooms are on the second floor of your home, it makes sense to have them on a separate heating zone controlled by an independent thermostat. This gives you control over heating dollars. Hot water pipes or hot-air ducts should not travel along cold outside walls where heat will be lost before it gets where you need it.

Expect one free callback for fine-tuning the system. Quality contractors will come back until the system operates properly. Don't get nickled and dimed to death with service calls because your contract does not have a method of verifying efficiency. Modern furnaces should operate at 80 percent efficiency (the other 20 percent goes up the flue). Don't accept upgrading or conversion work that won't bring your system to at least 75 percent of its input rating. DOE studies show that improving energy efficiency from 50 to 80 percent (from awful to optimum) saves $37.50 per $100 of annual fuel cost. Paying for improvement from 70 to 75 percent efficiency nets only $6.50 per $100. At that rate it will take eight years of savings on a $400 annual fuel bill to get back your money on a $200 flue damper—not a thrilling investment.

On service work, you can measure efficiency by comparing before and after utility bills. Contractors must be more exact. They should measure stack draft (inches of water in a gauge), net stack temperature (400–600°F. on older equipment, 600–700°F. on replacement burners), the smoke spot number (0 is excellent, 5 is unacceptable), and carbon dioxide (CO_2) levels in the flue (9 percent is marginal, 11 percent is excellent).

EVALUATING WORK

Heating contractors should be able to talk to you in plain language. Energy-saving fever has produced a lot of technical jargon. Ask for translations. For example, your contractor should explain the basic distinction between BTU input and BTU output. Input is furnace capacity. Output is the actual, usable heat you'll get. Both numbers should be stamped on the manufacturer's plate.

Starting with the contractor's heating-load inspection, use the sources that follow to cross-check and evaluate all the important information a heating contractor provides. Write for a standard Heating Load Form from the Association of Home Appliance Manufacturers (AHAM, 20 N. Wacker Dr., Chicage, IL 60606). Ask to see the contractor's form, and compare the two for thoroughness and detail.

Check the contractor's recommendations with your local utility company. Many now offer a home-energy audit. You'll pay $15 to $20 for the service—a good buy. Also verify the recommendations with the appliance manufacturer. You can get third-party help on product and installation standards from ASHRAE (Committee on Heating Equipment, Systems, and Applications, 1791 Tullie Circle NE, Atlanta, Georgia 30329), and from the Center for Building Technology (CBT, National Bureau of Standards, U.S. Department of Commerce, Washington, DC 20234). The NBS has an informative booklet (C13.53:8), "Making the Most of Your Energy Dollars in Home Heating and Cooling."

To check up on improvement and service work on oil furnaces write the DOE (Office of Public Affairs, Washington, DC 20585) for publication DOE/OPA-0018, "How to Improve the Efficiency of

Your Oil-Fired Furnace,'' and the EPA (Office of Public Affairs, Research Triangle Park, NC 27711) for publication IERL-RTP-P-298, "Get the Most from Your Heating Oil Dollars.''

For gas appliances write the EPA at the address above for publication IERL-RTP-P-252, "Get the Most from Your Gas Heating Dollars.'' This neat booklet even has full-color pictures comparing the flames on properly and improperly tuned furnaces. More technical descriptions are available in "Guidelines for Adjustment of Atmospheric Gas Burners for Residential and Commercial Space Heating and Water Heating,'' available from the EPA, Library Service, Research Triangle Park, NC 27711.

For conversion work, take advantage of the competition between oil and gas concerns (sometimes their public-relations war gets virulent). For one side of the issue, contact the American Gas Association (they have comprehensive literature; AGA, 1515 Wilson Blvd., Arlington, VA 22209), and your local gas utility company. On the other side, contact the National Oil Jobbers Council (NOJC, 1707 H St. NW, Suite 1100, Washington, DC 20006), and your local oil company. Write a letter saying that you're thinking of switching fuels and that you want the pros and cons; make four copies, mail them out and then watch the fur fly.

Here's a final goodie. If you have a specific heating subject that you want to know about, send it with your request for information to the DOE (Technical Information Center, PO Box 62, Oak Ridge, TN 37830). They'll send you a title and source list of available information on the subject.

GRIEVANCES

Shut the door on anyone offering a free heating system inspection, a free energy evaluation, a free demonstration, or an energy-saving gadget on a trial basis. Reputable manufacturers, government agencies, dealers, and contractors do not operate this way. I hear of case histories where free, fly-by-night inspectors have cut the oil supply pipe and furnace wires. Even if the victim (usually elderly and single) gets rid of the guy before he socks them with an inflated bill for inadequate repairs, they're still left with a catastrophe.

Follow the Primer guidelines for complaints about business practices, and contact the Better Business Bureau, and your local consumer-protection agency. For affiliated members, contact the Mechanical Contractors Association of America (MCAA, 5530 Wisconsin Ave. NW, Suite 750, Washington, DC 20015), and the National Association of Plumbing-Heating-Cooling Contractors (NAPHCC, 1016 20 St. NW, Washington, DC 20036) or their local branches.

Finally, beware of empty, energy-saving claims. Anything promised verbally should go down on paper. If not, you're listening to the wrong guy. Remember, just as there is one sure way to lose weight (eat less), there is one sure way to save energy (use less). Here's a reasonable, reliable guideline (used by the DOE and other groups): you'll save between 2 and 3 percent on fuel costs for every degree of heat you do without. Turn the thermostat from 70°F. to 65°F., 24 hours a day, and you should save between 10 and 15 percent of your annual fuel bill.

Insulation Contractors

Insulation is a hot topic, a panacea for OPEC price increases, fuel shortages, and America's dependence on foreign oil. It's the password that opens up homeowner's checkbooks.

In older homes across the northern third of the country, fuel costs may be larger than monthly mortgage payments. What can you do? Well, the government is increasing FHA minimum insulation standards in new homes, and they want you to insulate so much that the Department of Energy has a program where utility companies participate in low-cost consumer loans for energy improvements, and the Internal Revenue Service will give you tax credits after the work is done. (Write to the DOE, Office of Consumer Affairs, Washington, DC 20545 and the IRS, Washington, DC 20224. Also ask the IRS for the Energy Credit tax form 5696.) The big insulation manufacturers certainly want you to insulate. They are churning out batts and bags of the stuff along with commercials showing that two layers are better than one. How can you resist such a hard sell?

Many homeowners have already been sold, and now have an ocean of insulation in the attic. Sure, you can overdo it, but it is important to add some insulation where there is none. For example, an uninsulated, 1,000 sq. ft. wall has an overall heat loss rating, called a U Factor, of 220. Figuring heating costs at $2 a gallon for fuel oil, the bill just for that uninsulated wall would be $246 a year.

Add 3½ in. of fiberglass insulation and the U Factor is 88, which brings the heating bill down to $140—a dramatic saving.

But there is a point of diminishing return, even in the coldest climates, where adding extra inches of insulation starts to cost more than the amount you will save on your fuel bills. Remember—adding insulation is not the only answer to energy efficiency, only one of the most publicized.

SERVICES

When you decide to add insulation in your home, be prepared for an onslaught of energy-saving technicalese. You will read it in brochures and hear it from contractors—everything from K Factors and perms to thermal coefficients and adjusted degree-day tables. Don't get too excited; it's just part of the energy-saving shell game that promises 10 percent fuel-cost savings with one improvement, 20 percent with another, ad infinitum. You can actually assemble enough booklets on energy-saving home improvements to suggest a cumulative saving of more than 100 percent. That would be a trick.

The key to using insulation effectively is the R-Factor. It expresses the insulation's resistance to heat loss. The R-Factor is stamped prominently on all insulation batts, and all bags of loose-fill insulation, by every reputable insulation manufacturer.

Insulation contractors, no matter what type of material they are selling and no matter where or how it will be installed, should talk to you about the R-Value of insulation, not its thickness. Adding 3 in. of loose vermiculite (R-Value of 2.1 per in., or 6.3 for 3 in.) is quite different from adding 3 in. of urethane foam board (R-Value of 6.0 per in., or 18.0 for 3 in.). The urethane job will be nearly three times as effective. Do not deal with a contractor who will not express the job in a final, total R-Value, or who uses batts or bags of insulation not marked with an R-Value.

Most insulation work is done on new homes, as they are built, when the walls, floors, and ceilings are exposed, and may not be done by a specialized insulation contractor. More often, it is just another step in construction taken care of by the general contractor.

In existing homes, adding insulation to areas where the framing is exposed (you can see the wood timbers and the spaces between them called bays) is a job you might consider doing yourself. On open framing, fiberglass or mineral-wool batts or loose fill (only on horizontal surfaces) may be used. Rigid insulation panels made out of urethane or polystyrene may be added over exposed framing as well, but should be covered with a fire-retarding material like ½-in.-thick gypsum wallboard (on the inside) or siding (on the outside).

Over closed framing where the walls are finished, the job of adding insulation gets difficult. The most common solutions—blowing in loose fill insulation or pumping in foam—have given rise to many specialized insulation firms. Remember that when dealing with a specialized company or contractor handling only one type of insulation, with the capacity for only one type of installation, that's the product and method that will be recommended. But there are alternatives on every job. Unfortunately, some specialty contractors will tell you there aren't. That's one reason for getting a second and third opinion on every job.

Adding insulation to closed framing presents another tough problem. You can't be sure where the insulation is going inside the wall. Some TV commercials show cut-away views of pumped-in foam oozing around electrical cables and plumbing pipes. But it can't ooze around a solid wood firestop. And if your home is well built, there will be firestops in all the walls. Access holes must be cut into each framing bay, even the small ones over windows and doors. And this can make a heck of a mess. A contractor can work from the outside by cutting holes along the top of your walls, or by stripping off a few courses of horizontal siding, and cutting holes in the plywood sheathing beneath it. From the inside, holes may be cut through gypsum wallboard. I've seen a lot of finished basements (uninsulated until the energy crunch hit) where the attempts to repair these holes are the first thing you notice when you walk into the room.

QUALIFICATIONS

Judging the competence of an insulation contractor is difficult for several reasons. First, stapling up batts or laying in loose fill is not a complicated job requiring specialized tools, special skills, or even much on-the-job experience. That's why this work has become a standard do-it-yourself job. When skill and experience are not very important it becomes easy for any enterprising worker to print up a business card reading Insulation Contractor. In this case, the best criteria for selecting a contractor are job cost, length of local business practice (everybody has to get experience somewhere, but don't let them work out the wrinkles at your house), and, particularly, the quality of the job estimate and job contract.

Specialized insulation contractors offering work on closed walls should be checked carefully through former clients. On open walls, you can be sure of the insulation protection you are buying, and verify the R-Value of the material as it is installed. The results are predictable. Not so with closed-wall jobs. The effectiveness of pumped-in foam, cellulose, or other loose-fill insulation can be accurately judged only following a full seasonal cycle when before-and-after fuel bills can be compared.

Check each contractor who submits an estimate with the local Better Business Bureau and consumer-protection agencies. Ask about the contractor's license (if one is required in your area) and liability insurance. Affiliation with the Insulation Contractors Association of America (ICAA) is a plus, as is a recommendation by your utility company. Local utilities generally have enough public-relations problems on their hands not to take on another by passing along a low-quality contractor.

PROFESSIONAL PRACTICES

Contractors affiliated with the ICAA are required to subscribe to a code of ethics. Many of its provisions should be expected of non-members as well. Again, technical skill is not the central issue, although the ICAA code and every decent contract contains a phrase about approved or quality materials being installed in a professional or workmanlike manner.

Other key provisions in the ICAA code are that—

1. No misleading claims should be made about eligibility for tax credits.

2. Claims of product performance should be substantiated in writing.

3. Insulation thickness or density should be explained to clients only as related to thermal resistance and a stated R-Value.

4. Any limitations of performance such as settling or shrinking should be disclosed.

5. The client should be afforded adequate time and privacy in which to make a decision about the contract.

6. All terms of the contract should be disclosed before any agreement is made.

The insulation contract should list a detailed job description. Phrases like "insulate attic" or even "fully insulate attic floor with fiber-glass batts" are inadequate. The insulation type, thickness, R-Value, facing material, and installation method should be spelled out. Job start and finish dates should be included with a payment schedule, total cost, and a warranty of insulation effectiveness.

Some elements of an insulation contract deserve special attention. The way they are phrased in a contract, or if they're not even included, should weigh heavily on your decision among several contractors' estimates. One is called a Waiver of Mechanic's Lien Rights (see the Primer). The contract should contain a provision that reserves final payment until this document has been signed and delivered to you. This protects you in case the contractor doesn't pay the material bill, for example, and the supplier comes looking for you. Receipts for all materials and labor (for example, if the contractor has to hire a carpenter to replace siding) may serve the same purpose. Never sign a job-completion letter or make the final payment until every loose end, even cleaning up the site, is taken care of.

Another key provision covers a cooling-off period (time to rethink the contract you just signed) for installment contracts, which is mandatory in a few states and some cities. Inquire at your nearest consumer-protection agency. You usually get three business days. If you do back out, a related cancellation provision should limit your loss to a reasonable amount, such as 5 percent of the contract price to a maximum of $100.

EVALUATING WORK

Evaluate the integrity of a contractor by measuring the advertising and sales practices you are exposed to against standards provided by the Better Business Bureau specifically for the insulation industry. The ICAA code requires adherence to these standards. BBB guidelines state that anytime R-Value, price, or thickness is quoted for insulation materials, the following pieces of information should appear in the ad in a "clear and conspicuous manner":

1. A statement that "The higher the R-Value, the greater the insulating power. Ask your dealer for a fact sheet on R-Values."

2. For urea-foam products, this limiting statement: "Foam insulation shrinks after it is installed. This shrinkage may significantly reduce the R-Value you get."

3. The type, form, and thickness of the insulation.

Write the Better Business Bureau (BBB, 1150 17th St. NW, Washington, DC 20036), and ask for publication number 24-138, "Standards for Home Insulation Materials . . . Advertising and Selling." It is complete, understandable, and worth reading.

If your contractor is providing loose-fill mineral wool or cellulose, federal government specifications require labeling as follows: first the R-Value, then the minimum thickness at which the material may be spread to achieve that R-Value, then the maximum net coverage per bag of insulation.

If your contractor uses FHA- or HUD-approved products, don't sign the contract—there's no such thing. Write the FHA (U.S. Department of Housing and Urban Development, Washington, DC 20411) for details on their minimum insulation standards in your area.

It is not advisable to deal with a contractor who says there are no problems with installing urea formaldehyde foam insulation. There are. Recent University of Washington studies of 288 mobile and conventional homes found gas emissions coming from the foam that were associated with complaints of illness from the residents. This is only one of many reports that document problems. If you are attracted to the high R-Value of this material, please check into these potential problems in great detail before installing it in your home. I recommend that you pass it up.

Finally, you should remember to check up on any contractor's claim of a recommendation by a utility company. And you can get a relatively inexpensive or free second opinion in the form of an energy audit conducted by your utility company.

GRIEVANCES

Problems with an ICAA contractor should be directed to the Insulation Contractors Association of America (ICAA, 905 16th St. NW, Washington, DC 20006). Also forward complaints to the Better

Business Bureau. They may be able to help; at the least they'll have a record on the contractor.

Since this is an unregulated industry, you have to be very careful selecting a contractor; it will take a few months to discover that the thousands of dollars you invested are only saving you pennies instead of a substantial percentage of your fuel costs. And by that time a fly-by-night contractor may be long gone. Ask the BBB and the contractor how long he has been in business in the area—the longer the better.

Landscape Contractors

Good landscaping makes a house fit onto the building site and into the surrounding area. An absence of landscaping can make a house look awkward and out of place. But there are other, more practical reasons for spending money on the site as well as the home that sits on it. Well-planned, properly installed and cared-for landscaping can shield bedroom windows from car headlights on the street; it can also reduce the noise level from the neighborhood, decrease the amount of time you spend on yard care, save on air-conditioning costs by shading summer sun, and save on heating costs by checking cold winter winds.

SERVICES

Now that I've made such a strong case for trees and shrubs, let's talk about your lawn. It isn't a small sideline of the landscaping business anymore. The lawn's care and feeding is and always has been an ongoing project for do-it-yourselfers—endlessly cutting, raking, fertilizing, spraying, weeding, aerating. But even with improvements in mowers, and a new breed of electric yard-care tools, taking care of a lawn, weekend after weekend, is not terribly stimulating. More and more homeowners are turning this job over to lawn maintenance firms that go by names like Lawn King, Lawn Genie, Chemlawn, etc. They advertise a lot. Most provide patented lawn treatments (some do it with patented equipment) five or six times a year, including fertilizing, controlling insects and turf diseases, aerating, seeding—almost anything except cutting and watering. Most of these firms are franchises (the "special recipe" Kentucky Fried Chicken approach to Kentucky bluegrass), but Chemlawn is not.

Back to landscape contractors. Members of the Associated Landscape Contractors of America (ALCA) specialize in one or more of these residential landscaping fields: reclamation (controlling erosion and the loss of topsoil), general residential design and planting, maintenance and lawn care (Chemlawn is an ALCA member, for instance), irrigation (installing underground lawn-sprinkler systems), and appraisal. Members of the American Association of Nurserymen (AAN) offer design and planting services, consulting services (advice for a fee), maintenance, and casualty appraisals (what you might need if the oil delivery truck backs over one of every species on your property). Landscaping is a profession that combines art, a sense of space and style and technical expertise. Landscapers must understand how you will use the area outside your home, and select and plant vegetation (from species of evergreens to varieties of grass seed) that will make it work efficiently.

Another group of specialists (many are members of the Irrigation Association) install lawn-watering systems. An extravagance at first glance (a typical underground system for a development house might run $1,000), a professional can design and install an automatic system that cuts your water bills by covering the lawn evenly, for a specific, limited amount of time, and during hours (like 4:00 in the morning) when there is no demand for water in the home, and the sun won't evaporate the sprinkled water before it seeps in where you need it.

QUALIFICATIONS

Members of the AAN must be active in some aspect of the nursery business, and are subject to peer review for approval. ALCA, with about nine hundred members nationwide, follows similar guidelines. Peer review consists of publishing the names and home towns of applicants in a monthly or quarterly newsletter, and waiting a month to see if the complaints roll in. If they do, ALCA, for example, asks several landscape-related professionals in the applicant's area to comment. Then their board makes an evaluation. No objections? No problems getting approved.

It's not very stringent. No exams are required, no special certifi-

cations indicating expertise are granted. However, every state requires a nurseryman to have a license, not because it's a technical
trade, but to keep track of dangerous insects and botanical diseases
that may be carried in the root bundles of plants and trees.

These licenses are granted, only after the professional has been
tested and evaluated, by the state department of agriculture. The
name of the agency varies in different states. In New York, for instance, it's the New York Department of Agriculture and Markets.
New Hampshire and Kentucky do not have independent agriculture
departments, so the license is granted and administered by the State
Agricultural Experimental Station. In Indiana, it's granted by the
Department of Conservation. Write the AAN (230 Southern Bldg.,
Washington, DC 20005), and enclose $3 for a copy of all the various
state regulations.

Specialists like a Lawn King dealer, for instance, will receive
training in the specialties of the franchise—the proprietary fertilizer
mixes, and so on. However, because they handle pesticides (every
one used must be registered and approved by the Environmental
Protection Agency), each dealer must employ a pest control operator (PCO), and he must pass a specialty state exam (on trees and
turf, or turf and ornamentals, for instance) to get a PCO license.

Sprinkler specialists, like many home-service contractors, may
need an occupational license in your area. That's only a license to do
business, and a way for the township to raise some money. They
don't have to be licensed plumbers, submit special plans to the
board of health, or produce other licenses or certifications. However, there are a few oddball cases. In Texas, sprinkler-system installers must be licensed by the state before they can tap into your
water supply. There has been a push on (naturally, supported by the
installer's trade association, the Irrigation Association) for similar
state licensing in New Jersey. In a few municipalities, plastic pipe
(PVC), which is standard for underground sprinklers, cannot be
used. In all cases, the contractor should agree to conform to local
building and plumbing codes.

PROFESSIONAL PRACTICES

Specialty contractors like lawn-maintenance dealers can tell you
exactly what each treatment consists of, what it does, how often
you'll get it, and what the charge is. It's very cut and dry. Don't

agree to a contract for a year's worth of service that can't be canceled. What if you move, or decide to turn your lawn into a pool and patio, or a field of wildflowers?

Sprinkler installers should submit a plan (at least a rough sketch) showing where pipes will be laid, and what coverage the system will provide, given the water pressure and rate of flow of water in your home. The lawn that's in place will have to be trenched in order to lay the pipes. Some installers clean up and replace the sod. Some don't. Ask about it, and get any verbal assurances you receive ("heck, you'll never know I was here" just isn't good enough) written into your informal agreement letter or contract.

Landscaping service that involves more than planting a single shrub should begin with an analysis of the site. The landscaper should list existing conditions like major trees, stone walls, well caps, and walkways, and then examine environmental factors like the direction of prevailing winds, natural drainage channels, and the direction and duration of sun exposure.

After the landscaper talks to you about how the area will be used, he will come up with a design. It should be presented using a plot plan (generally available from your local tax assessor's office or the building department) that shows the true boundaries of your property, and the house location. These details should be combined with a plan sketch (overhead view) containing a graphic display of the information gathered during the site analysis—arrows showing wind direction, sources of noise, drainage areas, etc.

Finally, all this information should be incorporated into a formal plan, similar to a house blueprint, drawn accurately to scale, showing true size, location, species, and variety of every element in the design. Of course, you may not like the landscaper's solution. That's a matter of taste. But if the plan is presented with this kind of thoroughness, the landscaper is providing high quality service.

EVALUATING WORK

Think twice about old-fashioned landscape designs—the typical, dense, foundation planting. It's a 1900 solution for houses with exposed foundations; houses aren't built that way anymore. Walls are now finished with siding or stucco very close to the ground. And dense evergreens hugging the house can foster mildew (that's when the white paint turns green) due to lack of ventilation and sunlight.

Landscape designs can look good and provide service for your home. First, any design should cover twelve months, not burst into magnificent peacock feathers for two weeks and disappear. Second, landscaping can be a gradual process (you add two trees and some ground cover one year, a row of bushes the year after). Landscapers shouldn't pressure you into an all-or-nothing deal. Third, consider these basics about serviceable landscaping: evergreens check winds and shade year round, while deciduous trees drop their leaves in winter, and let sunlight filter through. That generally means evergreens toward prevailing winter winds, and deciduous trees to the south and west for summer sun protection. An evergreen wind block, to be efficient, must extend well beyond the line of the house (as much as 50 ft). But a wall of evergreens will check wind for a distance eight times their height (a row of 4-footers will protect a house 32 ft. away).

For comparisons to landscaper's recommendations, contact ALCA for a nontechnical book on standard operating procedures, "Guide Specifications for Landscape Contractors," $2.50. Write also to The Lawn and Turf Institute (TLTI, Marysville, OH 43040) with a self-addressed, stamped envelope for "Lawns Across America," a booklet showing the nine basic climatic belts and recommended grasses for each. Contact your county agricultural agent, the cooperative extension service of the state university system (write the U.S. Department of Agriculture [address below] for details of the program and services), and the U.S. Soil Conservation Service (USDA, 14th St. & Independence Ave. SW, Washington, DC 20250).

For lawn-maintenance firms, evaluate each franchise as you would an independent contractor, as their practices and expertise varies. You can write Chemlawn (450 W. Wilson Bridge Rd., Columbus, OH 43229) for details on their procedures, and the branch nearest you.

GRIEVANCES

For affiliated members, address grievances to local chapters and national headquarters of ALCA (1750 Old Meadow Rd., McLean, VA 22102); the AAN (230 Southern Bldg., Washington, DC 20005); the Irrigation Association (IA, 13975 Connecticut Ave., Silver Springs, MD 20906).

Unreconciled grievances with nurserymen should also be directed to their state licensing agencies, although such agencies will be more interested in USDA concerns about insects and disease than in business practices. Follow the guidelines in the Primer and lodge a complaint with your local consumer-protection agency, particularly if it is responsible for issuing and revoking occupational licenses.

Locksmiths

You probably know someone whose home has been robbed. It may have happened to you. There were over three million burglaries committed last year—one every ten seconds. About 30 percent were in cities of over 250,000. But city or country, 65 percent were residential break-ins. The price tag? Over $1 billion a year—more than $500 per burglary.

I've interviewed a detective of the New York City Police Department's Crime Prevention Unit who has a special title. He's called a legal burglar. He's the guy the department uses to get past the locks and alarm systems of organized crime to set authorized wiretaps and do other odd jobs. Now you would think that professional criminals would have the experience to set up impregnable defenses. Not true. Detective G. (naturally, he's a little wary of publicity) told me of several jobs where he got past the defenses of organized crime in as much time as it takes him to get in his own front door. He's good. But professional burglars are good, too. They get lots of practice. Only about 15 percent of all burglars get caught.

SERVICES

Many locksmiths offer complete home-security service. Some specialize in electronic home security, a growing field. Basic locksmith's services include installing and repairing locks of all kinds; opening locks without damaging them, originating new keys or changing the keys and cylinders on existing locks, and improving the security of locks, for instance, by reinforcing strike plates in the doorjamb, or covering all but the cylinder keyhole with a tamper-resistant plate.

But many of the most common lock problems don't require a lock-smith's expertise. Doors and the jambs they close against take a beating, causing the bolt on the door to work out of alignment with the strike on the jamb. Check for loose hinge screws before you call in the professional. Constant wear, humidity, and accumulation of dust and dirt can also affect the cylinder mechanism. If the key does not operate smoothly in the lock, spray powdered graphite into the keyhole of the cylinder; it's available at hardware stores.

Most residential locks are easy to pick. And a good locksmith should always try this before resorting to an entry that damages the lock, the door, or the frame. If picking doesn't work, most keyed locks can be drilled out. Locksmiths may carry a small, battery-powered drill for this purpose. It doesn't take long as the system of spring-loaded pins inside the cylinder are sheared through by the drill bit. At this point, any key, and probably a thin bread knife, will turn the bolt. But then you'll need a new cylinder.

A qualified locksmith should be able to evaluate the total security of your home, not just the lock on the front door. You may be in for a shock when you hear his opinion, and if it really scares you, get a few other opinions as well. Some installers prey on your fears in order to sell expensive hardware.

Detective G. told me that a top burglar, given enough time to op-erate, can defeat any mechanical or electronic residential-security system. A burglar can dial your home phone (you advertise it, right along with your address) from a nearby phone booth, and when you don't answer, walk to your door to hear the phone still ringing. He knocks; no answer. The phone is ringing; you don't hear it because you're asleep or in the shower. Ah, but you say you have a security chain on your door. Even if the burglar picks the lock, that'll stop him cold.

Well, I hate to tell you, but I have literature that illustrates, step by step, how to stick your arm through the narrow opening allowed by the chain bolt, attach a small tack to the inside of the door right behind the chain-bolt keeper, attach one end of a rubber band to the tack, and the other to the bolt on the chain. Now I've installed many locks, but I have absolutely no practical experience with picking them. But I tried this maneuver and, sure enough, on the first at-tempt, as I pulled the door closed, the rubber band attached to the tack retracted the bolt. I could hear it slide along the keeper slot. I jiggled the door a bit, and the chain fell loose.

QUALIFICATIONS

The Associated Locksmiths of America (ALOA, 3003 Live Oak St., Dallas, TX 75204) requires applicants to be eighteen or older and to have at least two years of full-time service supplying, servicing, or installing locks. Applicants must also provide character references from local locksmith associations and business references from two trade-related distributors or manufacturers.

There are no standardized apprentice programs in the industry, although ALOA does offer apprentice membership. Some, not all, of their members are bonded. All should be able to produce a registered ID card with the crossed keys ALOA symbol.

Check the Better Business Bureau or local consumer-protection agencies and ask for recommendations from former clients, that is, if you're planning a security improvement for some time next month. It's a little different if you leave your keys at the office. You won't have the time to investigate qualifications. Whenever you get stuck, call the city or county consumer-protection agency or the police department to see if the locksmith's license is legitimate.

In most areas of the country, local ordinances regulate locksmiths. Los Angeles Ordinance Number 83.128 specifies that "no person shall engage in the business of locksmith, or practice or follow the trade or occupation of locksmith without a permit therefor from the Board of Police Commissioners." They require names, addresses, five character references, and fingerprints. Each permit has a registered serial number that must be prominently displayed in the locksmith's place of business. Each locksmith has to keep a record book of "the names and addresses of every person for whom a key is made by code or number, and for whom a locked automobile, building, structure, home, or store, whether vacant or occupied, is opened or a key fitted thereto." The code also requires locksmiths to stamp their permit number on every key they make.

Check requirements and permit numbers (most are renewed annually) with your local police. In many metropolitan areas, you can contact a special "crime prevention unit." In New York City, for example, this special unit is set up to answer all types of questions about home security. In fact, you can make arrangements for a police oficer (always ask for a long, close look at the shield) to come to your home, evaluate its security features (or lack of them) for free. Not every city does it, but it's certainly worth a phone call. What better advice could you get?

PROFESSIONAL PRACTICES

A good locksmith should be able to provide bonded, licensed services, in an emergency, and on new work. He should offer many options, and explain the advantages of several models from several manufacturers. Be prepared for large price variations, even for basic entry locks. The locksmith should explain the protection you get from a simple lockset, and from a sophisticated, costly system like the Fichet lock. (It has two different channels on the key and cannot be duplicated on conventional machines. In fact, only owners with factory-issued computer cards can order a duplicate.)

Most police departments recommend a dead-bolt cylinder lock. A lot of companies make them. If you get one, ask the locksmith about reinforcing your door and door jamb for a corresponding level of protection. You are entitled to detailed estimates listing the product, manufacturer, warranty, installation method, and cost, just as you would expect from a roofer or a painter.

If you're looking for a complete security system (a good locksmith should be able to evaluate the security of doors, windows, skylights, fire escapes, access from an adjacent roof—the whole picture), try not to get hung up on technical, electronic details. First, no system is burglarproof. Second, the ultra-sophisticated, whole-house, ultrasonic, microwave, automatic police dialer, button-and-bow systems can be so sensitive that the false alarms will drive you, your neighbors, and the police to distraction.

If you do get caught up in the Fort Knox syndrome of home protection, ask the locksmith to concentrate on door and window locks, and perimeter alarms. The idea is that alarms go off before the burglar gets in, and if he defeats the alarm, the locks make breaking in such an ordeal that he'll try somewhere else. The locksmith should give you a rundown on magnetic-contact systems (opening a window or door either breaks or closes an electrical circuit, which triggers a bell, horn or claxon of some kind), wired screens (you see them on storefronts), vibration alarms, pressure-sensitive door mats, and other perimeter sensors.

A locksmith who knows about complete security protection should be able to give you details about Operation ID (called Identifax in some areas). It's a police-approved program of engraving valuables with numbers recorded by the police (send them to your insurance agent, too), which has been successful in breaking the link between burglars and their fences, and, in turn, discouraging burglars from stealing marked merchandise. Many police departments (particularly in more rural, residential areas) participate in a help-your-neighbor system called the Neighborhood Watch Program. Your local police will be happy to give you the details if the locksmith can't.

EVALUATING WORK

Neatness is nice, but in this business keeping out burglars is what counts. Try to establish the locksmith's track record (it's a bit of a long-shot but worth a try) by checking his name and reputation with local police and home-insurance agents.

The locksmith should provide detailed specifications before you sign a contract. All electronic equipment should be UL listed (you can write Underwriter's Laboratories, 207 E. Ohio St., Chicago, IL 60611), and meet local electrical and building codes. Manufacturers' warranties should be delivered to you, and met or exceeded by the locksmith in the contract.

A professional who has been in business in your area for many years should, like the police, know what kind of burglaries are most common, and, therefore, the best protection against them. Ask him for details and trends, then check them with police. Nationally, FBI Uniform Crime Reports show that burglary is increasing in the daytime. The worst month is August, vacation time. About a third of all burglaries are committed by amateurs under eighteen years of age.

High-risk homes are visibly unoccupied (two inexpensive timers can turn lights and a radio on and off as if you were home). Houses on corners with multiple escape routes are more vulnerable than homes on cul-de-sacs or dead-end streets where a burglar could be blockaded. Ask the locksmith for an evaluation of your neighborhood and home, then see if it jibes with what the police tell you. And don't be bashful about walking into a police station. The police would rather spend a few minutes with you now than a few hours later filling out burglary reports.

Here's a final evaluation. You may have qualms about it; use your discretion. Talk to the locksmith. Set up an appointment when you're home—he knows you're home, and everything is above-board and out in the open—and ask him to break in—with your complete approval, of course, in writing if need be. But I would put a lot of stock in a locksmith who could arrive at the house, say hello, ask you to make sure that all windows and doors are secured as though you were away on vacation, then walk in within five minutes without causing damage of any kind. If the locksmith can do it, the burglar can too.

GRIEVANCES

For affiliated members, contact Associated Locksmiths of America, Inc. (ALOA, 3003 Live Oak St., Dallas, TX 75204). Or, contact the Better Business Bureau, local consumer-protection agencies, and the police licensing board.

Problems with products should also be directed to the manufacturer. But remember that no company or locksmith can guarantee to keep out burglars. If they install the locks and alarms you contracted for, and installed them according to the manufacturer's specifications, and a burglar still gets in, the locksmith and the company aren't liable for anything. You may be pretty disappointed with them, but that's an opinion, not a grievance that can carry legal weight or get you a refund.

Major Appliance Contractors

When your refrigerator starts clunking and turning fresh vegetables old before their time, do you start cursing the company that made it? If your dishwasher drops the detergent during the dry cycle, do you wonder how many thumbs the installer had? When your electric range trips a circuit breaker any time the recipe calls for more than 350 degrees, do you want to strangle the appliance repairman who has already solved the problem five times?

If major appliances start acting up a week after you purchase them, you have a right to scream. But you won't have to because you're still protected by a warranty. If they conk out after the warranty expires, years later, do you still feel short-changed? When you pay $750 to have a dishwasher installed (that's an average price for a quality product and installation), do you half expect it to last indefinitely? If you do, don't, because it won't.

Every appliance has a limited life expectancy: for dishwashers it's nine years; ranges, sixteen years; refrigerators, fifteen years; washers, eleven years; dryers, fourteen years. By comparison, the average life of a sewing machine is twenty-four years. Of course, you can get a gem that lasts twice as long or a lemon that's nothing but trouble.

The optional colors, digital read-out displays that make a dishwasher look like the cockpit of a 747, and a host of other goodies can make you choose one brand over another. But most buyers want three things from major appliances: convenience, reliability, and durability, and they pay a lot to find them. Americans spend about $8 billion a year on major appliances.

SERVICES

Sometimes appliances are included to sweeten the deal when you buy a newly built home. On existing homes, the major appliances may or may not be part of the deal. You have to check your contract. But new home or old, you can tell from the information on appliance lifespan that you'll be buying most of them many times over.

Major appliances are called big-ticket items. That means you won't buy them on impulse. You're more likely to think it over and comparison shop. So manufacturers and dealers put a lot of effort into sales, and carefully consider their advertising.

You can buy appliances (and get them installed and serviced) from factory-authorized dealers, appliance stores, and from independent contractors. You have to evaluate how each source provides the following services. First, consider selection. Do you get to see and hear about many models from many manufacturers? The dealer, salesman, or contractor should be able to compare the features of several models (capacity, operating costs, and more), and match them to the needs of your household. Each manufacturer has its own language to describe products. For example, one air conditioner will have a power-saver switch, another an energy-miser cycle. Ask for plain language translations of all the marketing jargon.

Next, check into installation. Is delivery part of the price or is it extra? Be careful of low prices intended to lure you into a store; you may get stuck with high installation charges before you get out. Ask for a breakdown of one-lump prices so you can compare product and installation costs. Built-in appliances may require some carpentry work—is this part of the deal or does installation of a countertop range consist of dropping it into a precut hole and plugging it into an outlet? That kind of installation isn't worth your attention, much less your money.

Will Rogers said he never met a man he didn't like. Well, I've never seen an appliance that didn't eventually break down. This makes service important. Will you get service from the seller or will he take your check and run? Factory-authorized sales and service outlets have an advantage here. So does a local contractor who's been around for many years. A service contract may be available, for a price. At Sears, for instance, service contracts are pushed at the time of the sale, right from the first minute of your warranty protection.

A warranty is your direct link to the manufacturer. But find a dealer who can explain that "ambient temperatures" really means local climate, and that "the party of the second part, hereinafter referred to as the purchaser" means you.

Since major appliances represent major expenses, many are bought on time. Financing arrangements should be fully disclosed. If, like warranty language, the terms are confusing, and the explanations you get are vague, try another source.

QUALIFICATIONS

Local independent contractors should be judged by personal and professional recommendations. Check with former clients, local agencies that license home contractors like heating, cooling, and plumbing contractors, the Better Business Bureau, and your bank. Show them your financing agreement before you sign. If the bank can beat the terms, consider borrowing from it instead. Look at the length of local service; pick contractors who have stayed in business through years of sales and service calls.

Factory-authorized sales and service is probably the safest route. The problem is that manufacturers have a hard time monitoring just who uses these words in their ads. The Yellow Pages management sends lists to manufacturers of all their customers who use the phrase. But they do it only once a year. And some dealers and contractors are very cute about it. On one line, bold print announces "factory-authorized parts." Beneath it, smaller type lists sales and service. Of course, they can get parts for GE dishwashers only from GE, and that's not exactly factory-authorized sales and service. Always check the dealer with the manufacturer to be safe.

Manufacturers don't offer this relationship lightly. A case in point: Whirlpool brings people up through the ranks. They look for contractors, apprentices, and others who are familiar with the business. Then their local consumer-affairs office checks into the professionals' business practices before making a recommendation. Candidates go to school in Ann Arbor for several weeks to receive training in one of three product groups: laundry, kitchen, or refrigeration. To maintain this relationship, the dealer has to update his training periodically, and use the Whirlpool phrase, Tech Care. All his product literature must contain specific consumer information, including a toll-free "cool-line" for consumer services and complaints.

White-Westinghouse has regional training schools, and follows essentially the same procedures. They suggest that you ask if the factory-authorized service includes complete warranty work at no charge. Only an authorized dealer can afford to do that.

PROFESSIONAL PRACTICES

First, some practices to avoid. Be careful about hidden charges for delivery, different aspects of installation that are "discovered" once the washer and dryer have been delivered. Also, think twice about exceptionally low prices for demonstrators or floor models. There's no better way to sell a refrigerator with a bad compressor than to put a scratch on one side, then sell the scratch as the defect.

Other goodies? Rebuilt appliances; major appliances that are offered on a free trial like a $10 magazine subscription; and the "I can get it for you wholesale" routine. Nobody can sell you a stove or a water heater at wholesale prices. That's the price the manufacturer charges the dealer, who sells at retail. Do you know any appliance dealers or contractors who double as philanthropists by forgetting about profit?

A quality contractor or dealer should work to sell you the appliance you need, not the bell-and-whistle-loaded top of the line. If they pressure you to "move up" (Sears has the good, better, best angle), be careful.

For plumbing appliances, the contractor or installer has to check your water supply, the capacity of your water heater, and access to drainage. Ask about these details. If you have a septic system instead of a hookup to town sewers, for instance, ask about a dry well. Constant wash drainage could choke a leaching field.

For electrical appliances, the contractor or installer may have to provide an independent circuit. This is standard for refrigerators, ranges, ovens, and any other appliances that draw a lot of electricity. Like electric furnaces, 220-volt electric ranges require special wiring at the service panel, and a large, heavy-duty cable between the panel and the appliance.

Many installations may require the skills of several building trades; wiring should be done by a licensed electrician, custom cabinet built-ins may require a carpenter. A washer and dryer may rattle like a small thunderstorm if the installer does not take the time to level them, or if they are placed on a flimsy subfloor. Make sure you know when the delivery and installation will take place, and all the steps that are necessary to prepare for the appliance hook up.

EVALUATING WORK

Check a dealer's or a contractor's recommendations of specific products against detailed ratings found in *Consumer Reports* magazine (256 Washington St., Mt. Vernon, NY 10550). These details are also listed in their annual *Buying Guide*.

Inquire about operating costs. On many major appliances, they can outstrip the purchase price in a few short years. The dealer should give you a thorough explanation of EnergyGuide labels that show how much the appliance will cost to run at various electric rates, and how the model you're looking at compares to others for energy efficiency.

See if the appliance professional gives you accurate energy-saving information. For instance, a gas oven with electronic ignition instead of the old-fashioned pilot light may cost more, but will cut gas consumption in the oven by about 40 percent (remember the pilot burns 24 hours a day, 365 days a year), by about 50 percent at the top burners. The self-cleaning feature on an oven may seem like an extravagance, but the double-thick insulation in the oven walls required for high-temperature self-cleaning makes these appliances operate more efficiently at normal cooking temperatures. An energy-saving refrigerator isn't energy-efficient unless it has 2 to 4 in. of foam insulation instead of the conventional 1 to 2 in. of fiber glass in the walls. There are more tips like this that you can get from your utility company and the Department of Energy (DOE, Office of Consumer Affairs, Washington, DC 20545).

Check warranty language with the Federal Trade Commission (FTC, Division of Special Statutes, Washington, DC 20580). An interesting booklet explaining the Magnuson-Moss Consumer Product Warranty Act, 1975 (written in plain language, not by parties of the first part) is available from the Better Business Bureau (BBB, Publication No. 25-136, 1150 17th St. NW, Washington, DC 20036).

If you want to get technical, try *The Handbook of Major Appliance Troubleshooting and Repair* (Prentice-Hall, 1977) to check up on the recommendations and procedures of servicemen. Check with the manufacturer as well.

Finally, don't buy appliances unless they are UL listed. If the UL (Underwriter's Laboratories, 207 E. Ohio St., Chicago, IL 60611) tag is found on the wire or the plug, that means only the wire and plug are UL approved. What about the motor? Ask. UL doesn't forget to put their stickers on appliances. If you have any questions about the safety of a home appliance, before or after you buy it, call the Consumer Product Safety Commission's toll-free hotline (800-638-8326, in Maryland 800-492-8363, in Alaska, Hawaii, Puerto Rico, and the Virgin Islands, 800-638-8333).

GRIEVANCES

Take complaints about financing and general business practices to local consumer-protection agencies, the Better Business Bureau, and the local agencies that license home contractors. Always get the manufacturer involved, particularly over problems with a warranty. Many national manufacturers have active consumer-service departments. They may not give you everything you want, but in many cases they will protect their image at the expense of a dealer. Some have toll-free numbers where you can get the name of the nearest factory-authorized dealer, information about products and services, and action on complaints. Here are a few:

Whirlpool Corporation: 800-253-1301 (800-632-2243 in Michigan), working twenty-four hours a day

Maytag Corporation: 800-228-9445 in Iowa, Missouri, Oklahoma, South Dakota, and Wyoming; or write their headquarters (403 W. 4th St., N. Newton, IA 50208; 515-792-7000)

White-Westinghouse Corporation: 800-245-0600 (800-242-0580 in Pennsylvania), working twenty-four hours a day

Admiral: 309-827-0002 for complaints and dealers

General Electric: Appliance Park, Louisville, KY 40225 (502-452-4108)

If all else fails try the Major Appliance Consumer Action Panel at the Association of Home Appliance Manufacturers (AHAM, 20 N. Wacker Dr., Chicago, IL 60606, 312-984-5858). They are highly respected by manufacturers and consumer advocates alike. Their board, which consists of consumer experts as well as manufacturers, mediates serious complaints with dealers, installers or contractors handling refrigerators, freezers, ranges, ovens, microwave ovens, washers, dryers, dishwashers, water heaters, garbage disposals, trash compactors, humidifiers, and dehumidifiers. Contact them only after you have come to a dead end with the appliance professional.

Masons

Masonry is probably the oldest organized building trade. While science and technology have revolutionized many construction crafts, brick and stone are still set by hand, in a bed of mortar that's spread by hand, one piece at a time. It's ironic that the building trade which may have changed the least over thousands of years continues to produce the most durable structures.

Throughout history, when the rich and powerful decided to build monuments that would represent their greatness for posterity, they built them of masonry. The clean lines of Egyptian pyramids may have worn over centuries of slow, steady, natural sandblasting, but the structures survive.

The permanence and prestige of masonry is still with us. The expense has made it unusual on today's development homes, but not on public buildings. Schools may be steel framed but the walls are masonry because they won't burn. Attached housing framed with wood and covered with wood siding generally requires a masonry fire wall between units. In many condominiums, multiple-unit shopping centers, and other structures, these masonry walls have prevented localized, controllable fires from spreading into uncontrollable catastrophes.

Brick, stone, and concrete are exceptionally strong: they won't burn, they won't normally crack, split or warp like wood, and you don't have to paint them every few years. The crushing strength of good brick and stone is about 7,000 lbs. per square inch. This means you could build a 1-ft.-wide brick wall 1,000 ft. high, and the bottom layer of brick wouldn't break under the tremendous weight. In fact, the wall would be applying less than 25 percent of the weight required to crush the first course of brick.

SERVICES

Masonry is a general term. It includes several operations: pouring concrete, laying concrete block, laying brick; building fireplaces, patios, and stone walls. Some masons are comfortable doing any kind of work with masonry and mortar. But you're not likely to find one like that under the age of thirty (most apprentices start work at 18 straight out of high school) because each specialty takes time to master.

Many contractors fall into one of two categories: they do rough, structural masonry like foundations, footings, and concrete floors or finish masonry like stone façades, brick patios, and fieldstone fireplaces. Many of the tools and techniques are the same for rough and finish masonry. And a concrete contractor, for example, ought to be able to lay a brick façade across the front of your house. The point is, he may do a decent job on the brick, but not the expert job he'll do on the foundation.

Masons who build foundations are responsible for the most important set of dimensions on the job. Many masons carry a transit in their truck. This is a precise, optical surveying instrument used to lay out the house foundation accurately. On very small additions, you can get by with rulers, but not on major additions or new homes. Masons may get some help from the general contractor or, in some cases, a supervising architect or engineer, but it's their job to put the foundation walls in the right place. If they're off, the framers, carpenters, Sheetrockers, roofers, and every other trade that follows will be off, too.

Some of these contractors, called cement masons by the Associated General Contractors of America (AGCA, 1957 E. St. NW, Washington, DC 20006), have the equipment necessary to do their own excavating work as well. For residential work, a small bulldozer for grading, a back hoe for digging and trenching, and a dump truck for hauling fill, topsoil, gravel and other materials, will take care of all but highly unusual field conditions. In some cases, the general contractor in charge of the project hires an excavation subcontractor to do the work before the mason starts.

After the digging and measuring is done, the mason should be able to build forms to hold the concrete (again, sometimes with help from the G.C., or he may use rented, prefabricated forms); to structurally reinforce the foundation with metal rods called rebars, and concrete floors with wire mesh; to finish the surface (called floating on floors); and apply waterproofing materials. Foundation walls of a home may be all poured concrete, or concrete block, laid just like bricks, on top of a concrete footing. Similar materials and skills are used to make sidewalks and driveways.

Masons who specialize in finish work handle materials like brick and a wide variety of stone. This is the kind of mason you need if you want to add a fireplace to an existing home, build a flagstone patio, or brick veneer the front of your house. But all masonry is heavy. You can't plunk down a chimney in the corner of your living room without making provision for the tremendous extra weight on the floor. That means building footings and foundations. So your best bet is to hire a mason who has wide building and finishing experience.

QUALIFICATIONS

Cement masons generally serve a two-year apprenticeship coupled with limited classroom instruction. Bricklayers and masons concentrating on finish work may serve an extra year. The only way to get good at masonry work is to practice alongside an experienced contractor for several years.

Affiliation with the Mason Contractors Association of America is a plus, but your best assurance of quality work will come from former clients. Masonry takes a while to show the most serious effects of inferior craftsmanship. Cosmetic surface cracks can be repaired. Deep, structural cracks are almost impossible to fix. You can cover them up with mortar or stucco temporarily, but fractures can't be corrected with cosmetic surgery.

Put a lot of stock in recommendations given by architects and general contractors. Ask if they have used the mason over a period of time, on jobs like the one you are planning. Longevity is important.

If you have questions about materials or procedures that a mason recommends in an estimate, contact the Portland Cement Association (PCA, 5420 Old Orchard Rd., Skokie, IL 60077) and ask for their catalogue, "Your Guide to Cement and Concrete." It contains hundreds of different references to information on masonry products and installations.

PROFESSIONAL PRACTICES

A mason is one of the first contractors on the job. If you have a contract with a general contractor it should contain a provision that gives you the right to approve or disapprove of the G.C.'s subcontractors. But unless the mason subcontractor (sub for short) shows up in a suit and tie or dead drunk, don't rock the boat. All the subs are responsible to the G.C. who's responsible to you. If you insist on your own mason, for example, a lot of the responsibility for his work will fall on your shoulders, bypassing the G.C.

But suppose a general contractor is attending to all the details on your home-improvement project. You still want to be involved, right? Well, if you have to pick one or two times to concentrate on the work and look over someone's shoulder, I'd do it at the beginning of the job (the formative stage), when the mason is literally laying the foundation for the work that follows, and at the end of the job, when the inevitable rough edges are smoothed and the loose ends are knitted together.

If you hire a mason for a more limited and specific home-improvement project, shop around. Let's say you wanted to build a stone fireplace on the outside wall of your family room. The masons you call in for estimates have to take a close look at the location, from the bottom of your home where the weight of the fireplace will finally rest, through floors and ceilings that may have to be opened up, to the roof where shingles will have to be torn off and new water-proof joints will have to be built with complicated flashing.

There are really several trades involved in this operation: masonry, carpentry, roofing, maybe even a little rewiring if the chimney interrupts circuits in the outside wall (don't let the mason do this part, even if he wants to). This makes it impossible to give a flat price for a certain kind of fireplace, regardless of where it will be built, or to give a price per foot of chimney. This goes for driveways, patios, brick veneer around your front door, and other custom jobs. Consider this: one of the most important things about a very heavy object is not the object itself, but what it sits on. Sounds like a strange way to look at the job? It's no stranger than saying one of the most important things about a bomb is where it lands.

A contractor who gets stuck on the bluestone hearth, the design of the chimney pot, and other points of style may not have the long-term, practical field experience needed to ensure durability. Fireplaces, patios, driveways, and brick façades that are not supported adequately are not likely to collapse before the mason gets out of your driveway. They'll look great for a while. But in time a phenomenon called settling takes over. The ground under the chimney footing or the driveway slab or the brick veneer starts to compress from the extra weight. Everything starts to sink. The mortar joints start to crack. Water seeps in, the cracks widen, and away we go.

Look for estimates and recommendations from masons that include details about the weight of the masonry, and how it will be supported so it will stay in one place. Wood-frame structures are a little pliable. They can shrink and settle a bit without fracturing. Masonry can't.

Whenever concrete is used, ask the mason to explain what the mix ratio will be (the relationship between cement, aggregate, and sand), and if the mix will be air-entrained. Let this question roll off the tip of your tongue as though it just popped into your head. It should raise a few eyebrows. (Air-entraining is a process in which roughly 5 percent trapped air is incorporated in the mix as an insulator against freezing and thawing damage.)

Estimates of concrete should be listed by the yard, *i.e.,* a cu. yd., or 27 cu. ft., of concrete. Expect the mason to order concrete from a ready-mix company. It comes in a truck, mixed, and ready to place. You'll pay for all the material on the truck, so this order must be figured carefully. Some waste is okay because the alternative of ordering less than you need can be a disaster. These orders are generally specified by the number of bags of Portland cement per yard. A five-bag mix is minimal. See if the contractor specifies a six-bag mix (a little more expensive but also a little stronger) for any work where reinforcing rods are added.

Any technical questions can be checked with the American Concrete Institute (ACI, PO Box 19150, Redford Sta., Detroit, MI 48219). Their 82 technical committees set codes for concrete in all kinds of building conditions.

Contract specifications for masonry work have to be specific. For instance, simply listing brick veneer is inadequate. Is it SW (severe weathering), MW (medium weathering), or NW (no weathering)? Common varieties of stone like slate, limestone, sandstone, and bluestone can vary in mineral content, hardness, and porosity. Price will vary if the material is natural (irregular), semidressed (cut to approximate size), or dressed (cut to uniform size). This kind of detail alters price and quality. Ask the mason for all the options. Check them with a masonry supply yard, a local architect or engineer, or the International Masonry Institute (IMI, 823 15th St. NW, Suite 1001, Washington, DC 20005).

Consult the Primer for guidelines on evaluating the business side of your contract and checking up on recommendations.

EVALUATING WORK

I worked on several jobs as a carpenter where the general contractor used a remarkable mason. He started early, like 7:00 a.m. He had two short beers for breakfast around 8:30, two or three more for a coffee break around 10:00, and by lunchtime, everyone stopped counting. Every job was the same. And on one addition the foundation was laid out after lunch. It was a bit out of square, and we had to compensate for the mistake (it's tough to rework a concrete foundation once it's hard) by shifting the wooden sills.

The G.C. used the same mason on job after job. Why? He built beautiful fireplaces that drew evenly, kept the smoke in the flue, and the water out; he built foundations that didn't settle and that were waterproofed so well they didn't leak.

Long-term performance is the measure of good masonry work. Get recommendations from architects and general contractors, even from mortgage bankers and building inspectors. But satisfied clients are the best source. If you get a chance to look at the mason's work, check for cracking, not hairline cracks in stucco that covers the foundation, but larger, structural cracks that follow the lines of concrete block in the foundation wall.

Ask about wet basements, a common complaint of homeowners, that can be eliminated by a thorough waterproofing job. Thick layers of hot tar are standard protection. Waterproofing membranes (some incorporate insulation that can decrease condensation problems as well) may be used where a high-water table or natural drainage on the site makes the basement a good candidate for a swimming pool.

On finish work, look for uniform mortar joints cleaned out to equal depths. You should not see discoloration from sloppy applications where mortar spilled over the joint onto the brick or stone surface.

On fireplaces, check the flashing (the aluminum, or, preferably, copper sheeting between the roofing material and the masonry). The top edge of all chimney flashing, whether a single, custom-made collar called a cricket, or individual pieces called step flashing, should be folded into a mortar joint between courses of the brick or stone. This takes a little more time, but it lasts. Some contractors (including some roofers and general building contractors) may try to get by with aluminum flashing tucked under the shingles, and laid up against the chimney in a bed of roofing cement. This is a butcher job. It won't last. It will leak.

GRIEVANCES

If you're working with a general contractor, and you have problems with the mason, don't argue with the professional who, although he's working on your project, is getting paid by the general contractor. The orders and the checks for subcontractors are funneled through the general contractor. That's where you should go first for help. The G.C. can talk to his subs in a language they understand, and in a tone that won't needlessly alienate them.

If the G.C. can't get the results you want, or if you're dealing directly with the mason and problems arise over work quality, use the leverage of a final payment (at least 15 percent of the job, preferably 20 or 25). Try to work out a compromise before the job is completed. Take disputes over business practices to local consumer-protection agencies that license home-construction and -improvement contractors. For affiliated members, contact the Mason Contractors Association of America (MCAA, 208 S. LaSalle St., Chicago, IL 60604).

Painters and Paperhangers

Anyone can put paint on a wall, right? Interior painting and papering are the most popular do-it-yourself jobs. Over 40 percent of the $20 billion devoted to home upkeep and improvement every year is spent for painting and papering. And more than 30 percent of that amount is spent by do-it-yourselfers.

Basic painting and papering techniques are not complicated; they do not require a lot of specialized and expensive equipment. Appearance and durability don't hinge on your talent with a brush and roller. Good results are affected more by the condition of the surface you cover and the quality of the material you use. Even the best paint and the best wallpaper won't stay on a poorly prepared wall or a wall that has chronic maintenance problems.

Preparation is the real secret of quality painting and papering—it separates do-it-yourselfers from professionals. Sure, there are also little tricks of the trade that come only with constant on-the-job experience, but when you deal with a painting or paperhanging professional, you should concentrate on the areas that can make or break any job—the preparation and materials.

SERVICES

Some painters are only a cut above do-it-yourselfers. High school students painting barns in the summer may carry a hammer to drive in protruding nails, a scraper and sandpaper to get rid of flaking paint, but their surface preparation is pretty basic. At the other end of the spectrum, expert apartment painters will spend two days scraping, spackling, sanding, respackling, and resanding, even restoring old plaster moldings, and only one day applying the paint. Painting is the easy part.

You should not expect painters and paperhangers to restore seriously deteriorated surfaces. Rotting or split siding requires carpentry work. Plaster that is separating from supporting lath in chunks can't be saved with a little spackle, paint, and paper. Don't expect miracles.

On inside work, contractors should be able to repair all surface cracks in plaster walls and respackle nail perforations in wallboard. They should also be able to retape a wallboard seam, applying three independent coats of joint compound. On exterior work, small cracks, nail popping, and paint or stain deterioration can be remedied without help from other trades as long as the problem is literally skin deep.

As job specifications become more demanding, fewer contractors can be expected to handle the job competently. For instance, only some contractors have the scaffolding equipment needed for multistory exterior painting. Few contractors have the experience to handle inside work that includes refinishing paneling and cabinets in specific wood grains or that requires the use of exotic wall treatments like leather, foils, or fabrics.

QUALIFICATIONS

In the union, apprentice painters and paperhangers spend three years working under an experienced craftsman (called a mechanic), and attend weekly classes in subjects like mixing paint, applying sealers, setting up scaffolding, and other specialties of the trade. This should be adequate training, but in many union locals, cozy relationships with contracting companies who care about production first and education second have decreased instruction time.

Contracting companies pay high hourly wages to skilled painters and paperhangers, and some are reluctant to decrease their output by saddling their mechanics with an apprentice. These inexperienced workers get low hourly rates, and may be kept busy supplying a crew of 20 mechanics working on 6 different floors of an apartment building with paint, clean brushes and rollers, wallpaper paste, rolls of material, coffee, and more. I've done it, starting at 6:30 in the morning and ending at 4:30 when the last brush has been cleaned, and what you learn is what you see, period.

The upshot is that performance in this field can't be measured with a degree, a certification, or even an affiliation with a professional society. Your best bet? Get a recommendation from a friend who has had work done similar to the job you have planned. If you can't get a recommendation where you can see the work first hand, ask at least three contractors for estimates, and ask them for names of their former clients. You can't afford to be squeamish about these questions. It's not an impolite intrusion into the contractor's private life. A professional who has a good local reputation should be eager to give you several names.

On the job, look for small signs of professionalism. Painters who work regularly use heavy fabric dropcloths, never plastic sheeting. Their brushes are first quality, long-handled models with flagged and tipped bristles. And painters rarely work from the typical do-it-yourselfer's pan. Production painters work from 2-gal. buckets. Paperhangers will show up for work with portable pasteup tables, and may, for high-ceilinged rooms, use strap-on stilts for mobility.

PROFESSIONAL PRACTICES

Estimates and product samples are almost always provided free. When you have two or three contractors give you a price for the job, be sure you give them the same specifications. For example, if you want a particular brand of strippable, fabric-backed vinyl, ask each contractor to base the price on that material. If they have an alternative they believe is more suitable, ask them to price their recommendations separately.

Check any contract for a definitive description of the job area, how each area will be prepared, the material to be used, and the installation method. Generalities will not hold up in disputes. "The walls will be prepared for painting." What does that mean? Who knows. It doesn't take all that long to write out the particulars about spackling, sanding, stripping old paper, sizing walls, sealing raw wood, and more. Materials should be listed by manufacturer, type, color, and, if possible, a product number. This prevents the somewhat shady practice of substituting inferior products. Spell out all installation steps as well, such as how many coats of paint will be applied. A good contract should also include a statement covering the contractor's insurance and a completion date for the work.

On all cans of paint, the manufacturer lists an estimate of coverage, for example, 200 sq. ft. per gal. Get a similar estimate from the contractor, which should not exceed the manufacturer's rating (I'd consider that a maximum estimate of coverage). For wallcoverings you should figure coverage at 30 sq. ft. per roll, even though each single roll contains 36 sq. ft., because of waste in trimming and matching patterns.

Painters are reluctant to give guarantees because there are so many variables such as weather conditions and the age of the surfaces to be covered. However, a reasonable guarantee for a properly prepared, two-coat, exterior paint job is five years. Be wary of miracle coatings that have long-term warranties of ten or even fifteen years. Look at the language carefully—it may be so riddled with disclaimers as to be practically worthless.

Finally, don't expect a paperhanger or a painter to move your grand piano or your 750-lb. aquarium. Remove as many paintings, drapes, rugs, and other furnishings as possible before workers arrive. Everything you leave should be covered with drop cloths.

EVALUATING WORK

Among the hundreds of paint varieties there are some basic distinctions that may help you evaluate a contractor's recommendations. If you let the contractor know that you know something about the subject you'll always be in a stronger position.

Latex paints are thinned with water. Oil paints are thinned with turpentine or commercial thinner. The standard rule of thumb is to paint interior walls with latex, and both interior trim and exteriors with oil. However, the quality, durability, and hiding power of latex paint has been greatly improved in recent years. Its main advantages are quick drying time (nice for two-coat jobs), lack of odor, resistance to problems caused by application in humid weather, and easy clean-up. Vinyl- and acrylic-based paints are mildew-resistant as well.

Oil paints do have an odor, and take longer to dry, generally from twelve to forty-eight hours, depending on how much thinner is added. Many exterior oil paints have a chalking feature that allows the soiled, outer layer of paint to wash away in the rain. High- and low-rate chalking paints are available. The dirtier the air, and the lighter the paint color, the higher the chalking rate should be. For dark colors and very clean environments, contractors should not use chalking paints.

Consumers Union (CU, 256 Washington St., Mt. Vernon, NY 10550) has made tests and published extensive ratings of brand-name paints based on their hiding power, resistance to fading, and other factors. Write them for reprints of these ratings (for a small fee).

Find out the specific brand names of the sealers, paints, or stains your contractor intends to use. Write the manufacturer to verify the contractor's estimates of coverage and method of application, and then check several retail outlets to compare over-the-counter costs to the materials portion of your estimate.

Wallcoverings, like paints, are available in many different forms. Wallpaper, that is, actual paper, is not widely used today because significant improvements in durability have been made with other products. Again, you can judge the contractor's expertise by the accuracy of recommendations about the advantages of different products. For instance, vinyl-coated papers are not true vinyls, but they are considerably more durable than plain papers.

Lightweight vinyls, available in 36-, 72-, and 108-in.-wide rolls may be applied with conventional wallpaper paste. However, heavy-duty vinyls, available in 54-in.-wide rolls, have more hiding power on cracked and pitted wall surfaces, but must be applied with vinyl paste. If you redecorate frequently you may want strippable (fabric-backed) paper that can be removed from the wall surface intact. With peelable (paper-backed) papers you are likely to pull away the vinyl surface but not the paper backing.

For more exotic installations of foils, "wet-look" vinyls, burlap, linens, and grasscloth, it is good practice to recommend a liner paper, a relatively inexpensive, plain paper backing installed with butt edges. Exotic coverings are more expensive and more difficult to apply than are conventional papers or lightweight vinyls. And to protect your investment, be sure the contractor prepares the surface thoroughly. Surfaces covered with low- or high-gloss paints should be cut (scuffed up) with sandpaper to increase holding power, and the composition of conventional paste may have to be altered to 3 parts wheat paste and 1 part vinyl adhesive.

A final telltale indicator of quality is the way contractors create an unbroken pattern across obstructions like wall switches and outlets by removing the cover plates and applying pattern-matched scraps to their surfaces with rubber cement. It's a small but classy finishing touch. Wall switches can also be treated with a clear sealer to minimize fingerprint stains.

GRIEVANCES

Some painters and paperhangers may fall into the category of home-improvement contractors requiring licenses to operate in your area. Check with your local building department and consumer-protection agencies.

Specific problems with contractors affiliated with the Painting and Decorating Contractors of America should be forwarded to that organization at 7223 Lee Hwy., Falls Church, VA 22046, or their local chapters.

Your best protection, however, is a tight contract laying out the job in detail, and reserving at least 15 or 20 percent as final payment. Poor-quality work that doesn't look as good as you thought it would, or that doesn't last very long (the two most common complaints) are difficult grievances to settle. You can increase your chances of getting action if you include this phrase in the contract: "All materials and work shall be the best known to the trade." That means you paid for high-quality work and if you didn't get it, your chances of getting the contractor back or getting damages will be greater if this standard is included.

Plumbers

The Romans brought water into their city with aqueducts, and distributed it to their homes in lead pipes. (This trade gets its name from the Latin word for lead, *plumbum*.) In the Middle Ages plumbing systems were nonexistent. That's when plague killed an estimated 50 to 75 percent of the population of Europe and Asia in a twenty-year period. Sanitation was so backward that the first planned water system after the Middle Ages (in London in 1515) relied on some parts of the original Roman construction.

Water supply and waste removal are now strictly regulated by federal, state, and local codes. These codes cover where you get water and what you do with it after you use it. They also cover private and public sewer and septic systems, the kind of plumbing materials used to carry water and waste, how these systems are put together, and the professionals who do the work.

SERVICES

You may get water from the town or city. The municipality has its own engineers and plumbers to bring the water to your street. You may need to get water from your own land, in which case you'll need a well driller. In either case, from this point on you need a plumber to bring the water into your home under pressure and distribute it to fixtures and appliances.

After the water leaves the supply piping and is used, it enters the DWV (drain-waste-vent) system. Plumbers build systems that separate these functions (supply and DWV), eliminating any cross-connections that could contaminate the clean water. Each plumbing fixture is trapped (that S-shaped pipe beneath the sink where, if you're lucky, your wedding ring stopped instead of flowing out of the house). A constant level of water on each side of the trap permits gravity drainage, but prevents sewer gases from rising through the fixture into your home. Waste fixtures like toilets have traps built into their design. The vent part of the system (the short, open-ended pipes sticking up through the roof) permit free-flowing drainage just the way a vent cap on a Thermos jug lets the lemonade pour instead of gurgle out of the spout. All used water and waste products funnel into a soil pipe (commonly heavy cast iron) that runs out of the home.

If you get water from the municipality, chances are that it provides sewers (or will in the next few years) as well. A plumber can continue your system and hook it up to a sewer. So can a lot of other contractors who specialize in this work but are not licensed plumbers, and cannot work on the piping in your home.

If you get water from your own well, chances are that you'll have to provide your own septic system, too. Your plumber or other contractors (even your general contractor) can continue the system from the soil pipe to a collection tank for solids, then to a leaching field for controlled drainage of liquids.

A qualified, licensed plumber should be able to install, repair, replace, and maintain every part of this system from the water meter or well to the end of the soil pipe outside your home. You may find someone to handle supply or waste beyond these points, but in between, get a licensed plumber.

QUALIFICATIONS

The United Association of Plumbers and Pipe Fitters (that's the plumbers' union; UAPPF, 901 Massachusetts Ave. NW, Washington, DC 20001) has a four-year apprenticeship program (recently reduced from five years) supported by classroom study. Contact the

Department of Labor (Bureau of Apprenticeships and Training, 601 D St. NW, Rm. 5000, Washington, DC 20213) to find out if the plumbing contractor you're dealing with (union or not) participates in a registered and approved apprentice and training program.

In addition to getting professional recommendations from local architects, general contractors, the building department, and first-hand recommendations from friends and neighbors, contact the National Association of Plumbing-Heating-Cooling Contractors (NAPHCC, 1016 20 St. NW, Washington, DC 20036) or one of their 437 local groups. All of their members are Master Plumbers, a title earned after at least four years—sometimes five as an Indentured Apprentice Plumber ("indentured" is left over from apprentice practices in medieval craft unions)—and another five years as a Journeyman Plumber. Even then, only some applicants pass stringent examinations to become Master Plumbers.

Plumbers need a license to work on the supply and DWV systems in your home. Currently twenty-three states have a state plumbing board that tests and licenses journeyman plumbers. In other states, particularly in and around metropolitan areas, licensing may be handled by a county or even a township plumbing board. As a general rule, the thinner the population gets, the easier it is to get a license. If you can't find a phone book listing for a board in your area, call the building department, health department, local environmental and consumer-protection agencies to find out what kind of license is required, and who issues it.

In almost all areas, contractors who offer plumbing specialties like sewer hook-ups and septic system construction do not have to be licensed plumbers. These contractors are more likely to have what's called an occupational license (a license to do business, and a way for towns to collect money) that usually does not guarantee expertise.

Ask for this license (it should be noted on any contract) but, more importantly, ask how long the contractor has had it. Here's why. In many areas, even densely populated suburbs, these contractors may only have to pay a fee and fill out an application to get an occupational license from the local consumer agency. A fresh license won't have complaints filed against it—at least not yet. It takes at least three months to revoke a license and sometimes as much as a year.

In the course of taking care of your plumbing system you may also deal with a very specialized contractor like a sewer and drain cleaner. My advice is to check into specialty firms, like the local Roto-

Rooter man, carefully. A nationally franchised name may be only that—a name, with a lot of advertising behind it. Practices, expertise, and professional standards vary from firm to firm. I talked to one Roto-Rooter firm that responded to all my questions about a number of consumer issues, and another, a large operation on the East Coast, where the manager wanted all the questions in writing, and actually refused to give me the phone number of Roto-Rooter headquarters. I talked to the headquarters in Iowa, asking about uniform standards, central training programs, grievance procedures, and how they monitor franchised operations. Their representative told me only, "We keep track of them as best we can." So you should evaluate these and similar franchised firms thoroughly, as you would an autonomous, independent contractor.

PROFESSIONAL PRACTICES

On new construction the plumber works for your general contractor. The G.C. bases his price to you, in part, on an estimate the plumber gave him. In this case, the G.C. is responsible for permits, inspections, and the quality of work. It is standard practice to conduct a water test (sometimes called a vent test) on all new systems before the framed walls are closed in. Here's how it works: first, the plumber plugs up the soil pipe (the final disposal pipe). He then takes a hose up on the roof, turns on the water, empties it into a vent pipe until the entire piping system fills with water, and then inspects all the pipes and joints for leaks. With sweated, copper piping (that's the most common) it's not unusual to find a pinhole or two. That doesn't mean your plumber is no good. The fact that he made the test, found the pinholes, and fixed them means he is good at his job, and thorough.

On work where you make a contract directly with the plumber, it should include his license number, assurances of property damage and personal-liability insurance, detailed descriptions and costs of all labor and materials, assurances of code-approved work, and a guarantee for at least one year. If you deal with a large firm, ask who will be doing the installation. You may talk to a journeyman or a master plumber, then find three apprentices doing the work. National Association of Plumbing-Heating-Cooling Contractors' standards call for only one apprentice per five journeymen plumbers.

Contractors specializing in water and sewer hook-ups may not be licensed plumbers. In many areas the building department or another town agency will give you a list of several approved and licensed (that's an occupational license) contractors, who have posted a bond, and convinced local authorities of their expertise. You'll have to trust their judgment. You can make your own arrangements with the contractor about routing the pipes around your prize rhododendron, but you have to use a contractor on the list.

Installation of private septic systems is usually monitored by the health department or, in areas that don't have a separate health department, by the building department. It's common practice for the board of health to require a percolation test (drilling holes to establish porosity and drainage rates), performed by a licensed engineer (P.E.), an architect, or, occasionally, a surveyor. Then a plan for the system is submitted for approval. If it passes (it has to before you can get a building permit for the house), anyone can do the work.

EVALUATING WORK

Because the quality of plumbing can affect your health as well as convenience, there are many interested agencies you can go to for information and to compare the materials and work you get to approved standards in the field.

For new installations, contact the National Association of Plumbing-Heating-Cooling Contractors whose eight-thousand-plus members across the country are all master plumbers. Their national association is very responsive to consumer inquiries. Get a copy of the Uniform Plumbing Code from the International Association of Plumbing and Mechanical Officers (IAPMO, 5032 Alhambra Ave., Los Angeles, CA 90032). Go into your local building department, and, for sewer and septic systems, your health department. I've found that in almost all cases these local officials are not out to split hairs or nickel and dime you to death with inspections, and fees, and changes, and needless hassles. Most live and work in the same town your home is in, and take the job of protecting you from unsound or unsafe building materials and construction very seriously.

If you're interested in a wide range of technical and consumer information on home plumbing, direct requests to:

1. HUD, Library and Information Division (451 7th St. SW, Washington, DC 20410)

2. EPA, Office of Public Affairs (401 M St. SW, Washington, DC 20460)

3. Plumbing-Heating-Cooling Information Bureau (35 E. Wacker Dr., Chicago, IL 60601)

4. Plumbing and Drainage Institute, particularly for sewers laid in residential developments as opposed to private septic systems (5342 Boulevard Pl., Indianapolis, IN 46208).

Finally, ask your plumbing contractor a hypothetical question. Suppose, just suppose, that the excellent work develops a leak. Will he come back and fix it, at no charge, a year, even two years later? Quality contractors generally will, because providing this kind of service gets them the recommendations that wind up putting food on the table.

GRIEVANCES

For master plumbers affiliated with the NAPHCC, you can contact their grievance committee, or work through their third-party agreement. This option may be exercised for unreconcilable differences, and involves an independent contractor of at least equal stature and expertise to yours, who mediates the dispute. Generally, they come up with a compromise within thirty days, which is a lot better than you'll do in court.

For any licensed contractor (either a journeyman plumber or a specialty contractor) you can apply pressure at the licensing agency. In the case of specialty contractors, complaint registration has a cumulative effect, and can get their licenses revoked. This is a powerful incentive to bargain in good faith, and to make the client (that's you) satisfied enough not to lodge a serious complaint.

For licensed plumbers, go to the plumbing board at state or local levels, and to the building department. If the work you got is not the work represented on plans, the building inspector can verify the discrepancy. Also consult the Primer for general guidelines on lodging complaints about business practices.

Roofers

Did you ever stand around with your next-door neighbor talking about how great your roof is? That's the kind of activity you see in some TV commercials. "Hey, Jim, wait till you see those three-tab asphalt beauties I just put down!"

But nobody does that. Roofing isn't a subject for scintillating conversation. It's one part of your home that just lies there, without maintenance, until something goes wrong. Why? Because a new asphalt shingle roof (and that's what's on more than 80 percent of the homes in this country) should last ten to fifteen years. You don't have to reroof the way you have to repaint. And if heavy-duty shingles are installed by a real pro on a home in a moderate climate, the roof is likely to keep out the rain for twenty-five years or longer.

SERVICES

On new construction, some roofing work is handled by the general contractor or carpenter in charge of the entire project. I usually did my own roofing, particularly on additions where connections between the new roof and the idiosyncrasies of an existing house called for custom flashing, and one-of-a-kind installation. But on many jobs, new or old, this work is left to specialists—roofing contractors.

There are many kinds of roofing materials, many shapes, sizes, finishes, and methods of installation. A good roofer should be able to handle almost all of them. I say almost because terne roofs made of copper sheeting, barrel tile roofs (semi-circular terra cotta often called mission tile), and the Rolls-Royce of roofs, slate, do require very special tools and skills. You also have to beef up the roof structure underneath them.

A good roofer should be able to install and repair anything else. On new construction, roofers start work after the structure is framed and the roof deck (usually plywood) is laid over the rafters. The roofer must be able to spread a double-coverage layer of felt paper (55-lb. asphalt-saturated tar paper), install copper or aluminum flashing around roof edges, vents, skylights, and any other interruptions in the roof surface, and lay finished roofing.

On homes where the roof line slopes at least 3 in. per horizontal foot, a variety of shingles can be used. But if it slopes less than 3 in. per foot, the contractor should recommend roll roofing (similar to rolls of tar paper, but much thicker and coated with granules just like individual asphalt shingles). Flat roofs must be covered with layers of heavy, saturated felt, sandwiched together with hot tar. To lay this built-up roof, contractors will bring a giant kettle to the job that cooks the tar, and keeps it liquid during application.

But every roof eventually wears out. And then you may need a different kind of service called reroofing. It's very much like laying shingles on new construction, except when you reroof, new shingles are laid right on top of the old ones. This can be done once, even twice, before the extra weight starts to cause problems with the roof structure. It's a straightforward job that should cost substantially less than a new roof that starts from scratch on the roof deck.

Finally, roofers can provide coating and sealing services that are intended to take care of minimal leaks and prolong the life of the roof. This idea is similar to waxing your linoleum. The wax takes the beating, not the linoleum. It's a tantalizing, logical idea; a low-cost job that could make your roof last indefinitely. It sounds almost too good to be true and that's the problem—it's not true.

In a few situations (to cover the seams on roll roofing, for instance), a liberal coating of roof cement can be beneficial. But with the exception of flat, built-up roofs, roofing is made up of pieces like shingles, not one, giant, waterproof skin. There is a good reason for this: constant exposure to the weather makes the roof expand and contract, and when that happens to a single skin like an asphalt roof coating, the skin develops cracks.

Coating your roof with the promise to make it last and last is the stock in trade of fly-by-nighters. For $50 you get five gal. of black, watery junk splashed around on your shingles. Low-cost, quick-fix roof coatings should be avoided, period. They have become the cliché of home-repair and -improvement ripoff schemes.

QUALIFICATIONS

On new work, starting from a wood roof deck, you don't have to be picky about choosing a contractor. You can find clear, step-by-step instructions for work like this in countless do-it-yourself manuals. (Write the Asphalt Roofing Manufacturers Association, 1800

Massachusetts Ave., Suite 702, Washington, DC 20036 for a free copy of their booklet "Good Application Makes a Good Roof Better.") On conventional homes (not Victorian palaces with domes and turrets) the work is easy to estimate and perform.

This doesn't mean you have to feel guilty about hiring a roofer to do the job. It means you don't have to make exhaustive inquiries into the contractor's expertise: concentrate instead on the business issues. How long has the roofer been in business in your area? Longevity is important. Poor-quality work would get poor recommendations and, over the years, would put the roofer out of business. Does the roofer have personal-liability and property-damage insurance? Will he affirm this in your contract? Will he start the job with little or no money down, and agree that most of the job price will be reserved as final payment, after every detail is attended to? Will his warranty of the roof meet or exceed the material warranty of the manufacturer? It's easy to check this. The warranty will be stamped right on the shingle bundle. If you can't find it, write the company; they'll tell you. Will the roofer guarantee a job-completion date in the contract?

These questions are important criteria along with references from former clients (long-term clients who can tell you how the roof has held up). More impersonal recommendations can be obtained from local architects, mortgage bankers, building inspectors, and even general contractors. They tend to find a roofing subcontractor who's good, and use him again and again. If the G.C. is a custom builder (building from one-of-a-kind plans, not mirror-image tract homes), the roofer who works with him regularly must know the business. Affiliation with the National Roofing Contractors Association (NRCA, 1515 N. Harlem Ave., Oak Park, IL 60302) is a plus.

Consider these two indicators of a professional roofing specialist. First, a quality roofer will have a shop, and a special tool for making flashing called a brake. With it, flashing can be custom made at a professional level. Tin snips and tar to cover up cuts and corners is usually the inferior alternative. Second, a roofer who works regularly is likely to have a special contraption called a shingle ladder. Shingle bundles are heavy. Load a few on your shoulder, make endless trips up a ladder to the roof, and your body yells for mercy. A motorized shingle ladder has a conveyor belt of platforms that do this job with engine power instead of muscle power. It's an investment that only serious, experienced roofers who intend to be around for a while will make.

PROFESSIONAL PRACTICES

Estimates (get at least three of them) can be made only after the roof has been inspected. On existing roofs, the contractor has to see how much of the granular coating has worn away, if the edges of the shingles are brittle, if nail heads are protruding, and if flashing has pulled away from chimneys. He must also decide if the shingles can be left in place under a new roof, or if they are so brittle or buckled that they must be removed. If areas of the roof are spongy, removal may be necessary so that new plywood decking can be laid. When roofs covered with wood shingles deteriorate, it is customary to remove them. Otherwise they might rot in the dark, damp conditions just under the new roof covering.

At this point, the roofer should consult with you about the characteristics of the new roof. There are endless styles and colors to choose from. That's a matter of taste. But the roofer should talk to you about weight and fire ratings.

Shingle thickness is expressed by the weight of roofing material needed to cover 100 sq. ft., called a square. (And that's how the job will be priced; so much per square, including materials and labor.) Standard weight, 205-lb. shingles (you need about eighty to cover 100 sq. ft.) are packaged three bundles to the square. By comparison, 325-lb. shingles, which are the same length and width, have to be packaged four bundles to the square because they're much thicker. When the bottom of the shingle, called the base mat, is made from fiber glass, less weight is needed to achieve the fire ratings and long warranties of heavy-duty shingles.

Fire ratings can be a crucial consideration in high-risk areas like parts of southern California that catch a steady stream of hot, dry, Santa Ana winds, or where a home is remote and hard to reach with fire-fighting equipment. Look for an Underwriter's Laboratories (UL) label. Class A, the best rating, is for severe exposure to fire. Class B and C are for progressively lighter exposures. For details about fire testing, flame spread, and ratings, write UL, 207 E. Ohio St., Chicago, IL 60611.

A roofing contract should incorporate the dimensions of the areas to be covered; all preliminary steps like flashing, tar paper, and drip edging (flashing that covers the roof edges); the type, color, weight, fire rating, and manufacturer of the roofing material; how many squares are required; and a price per square installed. Include a statement that the contractor provides his own personal-liability and property-damage insurance; duplicates of the material warranty; and a performance warranty on the roofing installation.

Roofing a house does not take very long. Once the materials are delivered, a good three-man crew should be able to tar paper, flash, and shingle a large, low-slope, standard development house in one day. Since the work doesn't take long, don't give more than 25 percent of the job price up front. (You really shouldn't have to give anything.) Never pay for materials that are not on the site, or for labor that has not been completed.

EVALUATING WORK

On straightforward jobs, there should not be a wide variation (like 30 or 40 percent) among three or four roofing estimates. If one is way off, disregard it. Your best bet is to pick the roofer who has been in the community a long time, and has provided several solid references. Selecting a contractor by price alone can be misleading. A study of roofing firms by Washington Consumer's Checkbook found price variations of 213 percent on the same job.

Prices can vary dramatically depending on the materials you choose. The *1981 National Construction Estimator*, 29th Ed. (Craftsman Book Co., 542 Stevens Ave., Solana Beach, CA 92075), an interesting technical reference, lists 235-lb., 12 x 36 in., three-tab, self-sealing, asphalt shingles at $43 per square, with a labor cost of $29.20 per square. By comparison, more exotic coverings like mission tile (about $100 a square) also cost a lot more to install (the NCE lists labor for mission tile at $135 per square).

When you pay for quality service, take the time to check these indicators of a quality job: flashing between roof and chimney or, on an addition, between the roof and the second-story wall of the existing house, should be installed with a back-up system called counterflashing—flashing for the flashing. When copper is used (it's expensive but the top-quality choice) seams should be sealed with solder, not with caulking or roof cement.

If you can get up on the roof safely, sight down a row of shingles. They should be in a straight line. Shingles with white surface granules that help reflect the sun's heat (just like wearing a white shirt on a hot summer day) should not be scuffed up from the roofer's shoes (some wear sneakers on white roofs).

Finally, put a lot of stock in a strong, plain-language warranty of performance. This should be distinct from the manufacturer's warranty of product life. The shingles may last twenty-five years, but how long will the roofer warrant the job against leaks? If one develops in two years or five years, will he fix it free of charge?

Toward the end of my building apprenticeship—the stage between carpenter and general contractor—I served as a kind of crew chief for a superb building contractor. We did only custom work. Most of it was modern design with a lot of open spaces and a lot of glass. On one addition job, we installed a 4 x 4 ft. skylight; they are notorious for leaking, no matter how careful you are. And sure enough, this one developed a tiny leak one month after we finished. The following morning we went back and fixed it. About six months later another leak developed. We fixed that one too. Over a year later the first pinhole opened up again. The next day we spent eight hours there, pulled out the skylight, rebuilt the flashing, and reinstalled it, free. It hasn't leaked since, and that was 1973.

Look for the kind of high-quality, long-term recommendations that are given only when a contractor honors his warranty, and is concerned about his reputation.

GRIEVANCES

For affiliated members, contact the National Roofing Contractors Association (NRCA, 1515 N. Harlem Ave., Oak Park, IL 60302). For complaints about roofing products contact the Asphalt Roofing Manufacturer's Association (ARMA, 1800 Massachusetts Ave., Suite 702, Washington, DC 20036).

For serious, unreconciled complaints, go to your local consumer-protection agency. In some areas roofers need a license to operate as home contractors. Your complaints can put this license in jeopardy. If you encounter problems with the warranty (say, the roofer won't come back to fix leaks), call the roofing manufacturer—most are national companies in hot competition with each other. They can't afford to have a poor installation take the name of their product into the mud along with the contractor's reputation. Write them and get them involved.

Your ace in the hole is the large final payment. This is powerful leverage. Use it to help solve grievances before the job is completed.

Solar Contractors

I've gone to a lot of home-trade shows, those events held at Mc-Cormack Place in Chicago, the Colosseum in New York, and other places large enough to display the wares of thirty siding manufacturers, forty companies that make bathroom fixtures, and just about everything else you can find in, on, or near a home.

I first noticed in 1974 that, at many shows, solar-equipment manufacturers needed an entire aisle to themselves. They were offering gadgets like solar cigarette lighters, and intricate, innovative, high-technology equipment like Fresnel lens, concentrating-mirror collectors that track the sun across the sky. I also started to see solar products that can only be characterized as the ultimate in poor design and shabby construction. Some companies were selling flat plate collectors (the boxes filled with pipes that lie on a house roof facing the sun) that were nothing more than large-scale cookie pans covered with plastic wrap.

As energy prices increased, the number of solar-equipment manufacturers and installers did also. Today, with fuel oil on a short road to $2 a gal., few homes are completely solarized—in most solar homes conventional heating and cooling systems have to be installed as back-ups for cloudy days. Storage is still a problem. When the sun is out, many solar systems, even primitive ones, can provide enough heat and hot water; but storing enough energy to keep you going during several dark days requires a lot of space and investment. Solar energy can be converted directly to electricity using silicone-based, photovoltaic cells. But this process, which requires battery storage, is still too expensive and too inefficient for widespread residential use.

The solar industry is still in its infancy. Some optimists think it can end our dependence on oil, but Department of Energy studies project that only 7 percent of the country's energy needs will be met with solar power by the year 2000—not exactly the wave of the near future. But when you can buy a quick-recovery electric water heater for $250, and (at 6 cents per Kwh) pay an average of $288.66 to operate it for one year, solar energy starts to look more and more promising.

SERVICES

Solar systems are still largely experimental, the way television was thirty-five years ago. Finding a qualified serviceman is difficult. There are some thirty-five hundred solar suppliers and installers across the country, and most of them are new to the business.

Experienced solar contractors must combine practical, technical, and theoretical skills to evaluate all the complex variables of solar space and water heating installations. They have to analyze how your home is oriented for sun exposure at different hours of the day in different seasons. They have to compute heating and cooling loads, decipher degree day tables, sun angles, and weather data, and match these requirements to the right solar equipment. That's tough enough. But on top of this, they must have the plumbing and mechanical skills of a conventional heating and cooling contractor to install the equipment.

Some solar companies sell proprietary systems. But there are many choices. Active solar systems can use a liquid medium (usually water) with pumps and piping, or air with fans and ductwork. Contractors who sell liquid systems can incorporate their operation with conventional appliances, but for space heating they have to find room for a 600- to 1,000-gal. storage tank. Hot-air systems can be combined with conventional ductwork, but require rock or gravel storage bins (that's how the heat is stored) roughly two-and-one-half times as large as liquid storage tanks—generally ½ cu. ft. of rock for every sq. ft. of solar collector.

QUALIFICATIONS

Solar contractors, as such, are not licensed. However, most firms in the field are not limited only to solar work. For instance, a new solar home is built from a set of approved plans as other homes are. Both the architects and engineers who draw up the plans are licensed and affiliated with professional societies that maintain codes of ethics, standards of professional practice, and grievance committees. Home builders and general contractors who have become "solar involved" will, in almost all localities, be regulated by a set of building codes, need a license, and be affiliated with professional groups as well.

Contractors affiliated with the National Association of Solar Contractors (NASC) undergo periodic evaluations of experience and performance to receive certification. This group, whose literature is refreshingly pro-consumer instead of strictly self-serving, maintains a Division of Consumer Affairs, a well-defined grievance procedure, and monitors sales representations of solar systems, energy-saving claims, contract-payment terms and conditions, financing arrangements, standards of workmanship, and warranties.

Other listings of dealers and contractors may be obtained from the NASC (Suite 928-910, 17th St. NW, Washington, DC 20006), and from the International Solar Energy Society (ISES, American Section, American Technological University, PO Box 1416, Killeen, TX 76541), and their thirty-plus regional chapters.

Listings of solar-involved builders and general contractors may be obtained from the National Solar Heating and Cooling Information Center (NSHCIC, PO Box 1607, Rockville, MD 20850), and the National Association of Home Builders (NAHB, 15th and M Sts. NW, Washington, DC 20005).

In addition to asking contractors for references from former clients, check at local utility companies. They regularly deal with solar contractors who connect installations to conventional back-up systems. Knowledge of local codes is important, particularly in some communities where solar installations may contravene codes governing façade appearance. In other words, the community doesn't like it when you put big black boxes on your roof.

If a dealer or contractor specifies brand-name equipment, inquire if the manufacturer offers technical and in-the-field support (many do). Be sure the contractor will offer regular and emergency service.

PROFESSIONAL PRACTICES

Solar installations incorporated in the construction of new homes are the most efficient because structural and mechanical plans are coincidental, and do not compete with each other. It is essential that the architect, engineer, or general contractor in charge of the project has technical and practical solar expertise.

A solar installation made on existing structures (called retrofitting) should begin with a thorough investigation of your present heating and cooling system, the structural and weather-resisting characteristics of possible collector sites, and the possibilities of installing pipes, pumps, or ductwork without ripping down half the house.

Installation practices vary widely, but you can check a specific, proposed application with the NASC, the NSHCIC, and the Solar Energy Research Institute (SERI, 1617 Cole Blvd., Golden, CO 80401). All contractors should meet the Minimum Standards for Solar Heating and Domestic Hot Water Systems (on the job and in the contract). Write for a copy of these standards to: National Bureau of Standards, Solar Technology Group (Bldg. 225, Washington, DC 20234) or to the NSHCIC.

Beware of solar salespeople, dealers, and manufacturers who gut warranties and performance data with disclaimers like this: "The XYZ collector requires installation by skilled professionals whose practices are at their own discretion and risk. Consequently, XYZ Collector Company can take no responsibility for the installation or performance of the system." It could blow up, or grow fangs and attack your cat, but they're not responsible.

The most useful collection of practical, up-to-date information on the latest solar products and techniques is called the "Solar Energy Information Locator," a free product of the Solar Energy Research Institute. It's worth writing for.

EVALUATING WORK

Inquire if the solar contractor is affiliated with the National Association of Solar Contractors or the International Solar Energy Society, if he is certified or licensed to operate in your area, if he deals with manufacturers who offer technical assistance, and will install systems to perform at or above these standards.

Solar installations are technically complex. If you ask the contractor a lot of questions you're likely to get answers laced with solar technicalese that won't make much sense to you. Ask for explanations in plain language. Don't let any contractor or salesman hide problems behind scientific product descriptions or gobbledegook charts and graphs. If you do want to do some technical comparison shopping, write for the *Solar Engineering Master Catalog,* a comprehensive listing of products and specifications (for $11) from: Solar Energy Industries Association (SEIA, 1001 Connecticut Ave., Washington, DC 20036).

A knowledgeable dealer or contractor should also be able to inform you about solar tax exemptions. A state-by-state breakdown is available from the NSHCIC detailing federal maximums, and the states offering combinations of property, income, and sales-tax exemptions. California, Montana, and Massachusetts currently reduce state credits when a federal credit is taken.

Finally, inquire about testing procedures. Typically, solar systems should be pressure-tested for possible leaks, and thermometers should be placed on pipes or air ducts running to and from the collector source to determine heat gain. The entire system should be efficiently cycled (this may take a few days of fine-tuning), and every installation must include some method of monitoring performance.

GRIEVANCES

For affiliated members, ask the NASC for their Solar Complaint Form, or direct complaints to the ISES. I have to pause here to salute the NASC for putting together a consumer-complaint form and having the guts to publicize it. It would be easy to interpret this the wrong way, *i.e.*, they must be expecting the complaints to flow like water if they have a form all printed up, ready and waiting. But I think it's great. Few associations or professional societies are this realistic and straightforward about a basic consumer question: who will help me out if problems develop?

You can get sources for more help in the SERI "Solar Energy Information Locator." It lists several consumer groups as well as every state energy office, energy extension service (state level offices of the Department of Energy), and state solar offices, which have been established in most states. Also, see the Consumer Information Sources in the appendix.

The federal government provides a wealth of information and services concerning solar energy—probably more than for any other specialized field of interest to home consumers. Write the NSHCIC (PO Box 1607, Rockville, MD 20850) for a rundown.

Swimming Pool Contractors

A swimming pool is a very desirable home improvement. Replacing an inefficient heating system or insulating your attic may be more sensible improvements, but they won't return your investment when you sell because buyers take these features for granted. But a pool is an obvious, luxurious extra—it makes the value of a home appreciate, and will probably return your investment if you sell.

Luxuries, however, are expensive. Pools, particularly in-ground pools, are initially expensive, and over the term of ownership, costly to maintain; you should consider expenses carefully before signing a contract for construction. An increase in the value of your home will be accompanied by an increased assessment, higher real-estate taxes, higher rates for homeowner's liability insurance, and increased utility bills for electricity and water. If you can afford the long-term costs, there are many advantages to owning a pool. One advantage I hear from parents is, "During the summer, I know where my kids are."

SERVICES

Before you talk to a pool salesman or a pool builder, check with your local building and health departments. Health codes may impose restrictions on piping, water supply, and drainage. Building codes may forbid certain types of specialized pool construction, restrict the location, and require special fencing.

Within these allowable limits, talk to several pool dealers and builders about pools that suit your needs and budget. This research effectively cuts off the high-pressure, high-price-end sales pitches used by some pool dealers, and also gives you a way to check the pool builder's knowledge of local codes.

If the dealer or builder represents only one type of pool, you will not hear much about its disadvantages. He's got no substitute if you're not impressed with the product. But there are many types of pools, many building materials and methods of construction. A good salesman should discuss the positive and negative features of several types so you can make an informed decision. In-ground pool shells can be made of concrete block, cement (representing 44 percent of in-ground construction), Gunnite, wood, steel, aluminum, and fiber glass.

A knowledgeable dealer or builder should also be able to demonstrate the most economical piping and heating systems, he should explain how to orient the pool to reduce heating costs, the advantages of strategically placed wind breaks that cut down on air cooling, even small points like placing the skimmer so that prevailing wind patterns push fallen leaves into it.

While many above-ground pools can be installed by do-it-yourselfers, in-ground construction requires excavation equipment, expertise in analyzing soil composition (one of the biggest problems with new pools is that they settle, and this causes cracks and leaks), as well as specialized construction and finishing techniques. It does not make sense to hire several specialized contractors (a mason, a carpenter, an electrician, etc.) to build a particular piece of the pool. One dealer or one builder should be solely responsible for the project.

QUALIFICATIONS

Pool building is a referral business. In-ground construction requires such a range of specialized skills that it is customary for clients to get the names of former customers just the way they would when hiring a general-building contractor. Pool builders should be willing, if not eager, to give you several names of past customers; don't deal with a contractor who is reluctant to supply them.

When you look for recommendations, do not overreact to the most common complaint about pool builders—the job took too long to complete. You will be paying by the contract price, not by the hour. Your family may be dying to get in the water, but be glad that a contractor will stick it out through the final, time-consuming details.

A knowledge of local building and health codes is an essential qualification for any contractor. Pool construction will require a building permit in almost all localities; plans must be submitted, and a building inspector must be satisfied. The length of local building practice also indicates the contractor's experience with local soil conditions and the water supply. Will the water need to be treated? Is there enough available during dry spells? Have other local pool owners been hit with special fees for recreational water use? These are a few of the questions the contractor should answer.

Referrals are standard operating procedure. But you can weed out building contractors, masons, and plumbers who do a pool only now and then (or who simply add a 10 or 15 percent middle-man fee onto the price of a pool contractor they hire) by looking for dealer or builder certification from the National Spa and Pool Institute (NSPI, 2000 K St. NW, Washington, DC 20006).

PROFESSIONAL PRACTICES

There is a big difference between a pool salesman and a pool builder. The salesman may promise the world; the builder has to deliver. Some companies actually have a policy that does not allow you to see the salesman after a deal is closed—the builder takes all the heat and explains all the little misunderstandings. Verbal commitments are meaningless.

Don't buy from a salesman who embellishes the contents of the company's written brochures. Believe me, they have already browbeaten their copywriters until every possible benefit has been highlighted. Don't buy if you are offered a special price because the company wants to use your pool as a showcase. This may appeal to your vanity (wow, they've chosen my home as a showcase), or you may imagine the extra work and attention to detail that will go into this "model" pool. It's not going to happen.

Don't buy from an independent salesman who says he represents many companies. First of all, no company retains salesmen who sell the competition's goods, and second, any contract you sign is likely to be peddled to a company that has trouble recruiting clients on its own. Never make out a deposit check to the salesman. If you are pressured, if a large deposit is required to reserve the pool or to line up the crew, show the salesman to the door.

You may check the company's references, but wind up selecting a pool type or style that they have not built locally. In any case, you can't order Model B from their catalogue the way you order one from column B in a Chinese restaurant: each pool must be built to meet the special conditions of the area. The contract must include the exact site of the pool, its dimensions in great detail, the type, grade, weight, color, size, and brand name of all materials used in its construction, and all specifications (including warranties) for support equipment such as piping, pumps, heaters, filters, and skimmers. The contract should list the final, total cost, including all work and material required to make the completed, code-approved pool operational. Watch out for add-on charges for cleaning equipment, tile edging, or a bordering walkway that appeared in the brochure but not in your contract.

All construction must be certified as conforming to local codes. Additionally, you can request that all specifications conform to the extremely detailed set of NSPI Minimum Standards for Residential Pools. It covers the relationships between depths and sloping floors, between shallow and deep ends, ladder and diving-board requirements, and more. Compare your pool specifications to these, and to the average size of residential pools: 16 x 32 ft., 3½ ft. deep at the shallow end, and 8 ft. deep at the other.

Pay particular attention to the material specified for interior finishing. Many combinations are possible: for instance, an all-steel frame covered with a vinyl liner, bolted panels of prefinished fiber glass, rough cement (it tends to trap algae), smooth plastered walls, and a variety of pool paints.

Ask about the resin content of the specified pool paint—the higher the better. Beware of any product that is called "rubberized"—this is a meaningless term often used to disguise inferior products. Pool paint may be rubber-based or, better yet, made of natural chlorinated rubber. This material is five times more impermeable than standard vinyl paints. It may stain slightly at the water line as floating oils (usually from suntan lotion) soften its surface, but it resists yellowing more than lower-cost, synthetic-rubber paints (styrene butadiene formulations).

EVALUATING WORK

The best evaluation is an on-site inspection of a pool similar to the one you are planning, and talks with several former clients of the pool dealer or builder.

There are several other ways you can judge the contractor's expertise. Compare the layout and basic specifications of the pool to code limits you get from the local building and health departments. Ask the contractor (and former clients) about establishing an access route to the pool site—how materials will be carried in, what protective measures will be taken for landscaping.

Also, inquire about operating costs. The American Red Cross recommends a water temperature of 78°F. Will the specified heater be able to maintain this temperature? Check on this. Most heater manufacturers can supply tables that relate heater capacity to two factors: the average number of degrees a pool temperature will be raised during the coldest month of use, and the pool-surface area.

Another important calculation is the filtering rate. Ask the contractor for the number of hours required for a full filtration cycle. Check this information, too. A maximum filtering rate will be stamped on the filter manufacturer's plate. It lists capacity in gallons per minute (gpm). Multiply this figure by sixty to get gallons per hour (gph), and then divide the pool's gallon capacity by the gph figure. For example: your pool will hold 36,000 gal.; the filter is rated at 15 gpm; multiply by 60 (equals 900) to get gph; then divide 36,000 by 900, which equals a forty-hour filtration cycle. Since a maximum cycle should be no more than eighteen hours (twelve hours is commonly recommended), the 15 gpm filter is the wrong filter. And it's possible that the pool professional who recommended it is the wrong guy for the job.

Check any water treatment information with your local health department. A free residual chlorine level of 0.6 to 1 part per million (ppm) is standard. Copper or iron traces from supply piping should not exceed 0.5 ppm.

GRIEVANCES

For affiliated members, direct complaints to the National Spa and Pool Institute (NSPI, 2000 K St. NW, Washington, DC 20006). Complaints about business practices and financing arrangements should be directed to local consumer-protection agencies. But try to solve disputes during the job. At this stage you have the leverage of a reserved final payment (leave as much as possible), and another powerful weapon, particularly in the pool-building business—the power to spread positive or negative recommendations.

Water-conditioning Contractors

Did you know that some water is soft and some is hard? When you catch water in a rain barrel, it's soft. When you pump it up from the ground it's usually hard. Soft and hard are the plain-language descriptions of the mineral content, particularly calcium and magnesium, in water.

Soft water is nice to wash with. It's silkier than hard water, and it gets you cleaner. Hard water can cause all kinds of problems. The Water Quality Research Council has estimated that when hard water is used in a typical household, it costs about $40 extra each year in soap and detergent use, $60 extra in plumbing repairs and replacements, $30 in shortened life of linens and clothes, and $25 in extra fuel costs. The total estimated cost to consumers is over $6 billion annually.

The scientific way to measure water hardness is by the number of grains per gallon (gpg) or parts per million (ppm) of minerals that remain undissolved or suspended in the water. The U.S. Department of the Interior and the Water Quality Association use the following hardness guidelines:

HARDNESS LEVEL	GRAINS PER GALLON	PARTS PER MILLION
soft	less than 1.0	less than 17.1
slightly hard	1–3.5	17.1–60
moderately hard	3.5–7.0	60–120
hard	7.0–10.5	120–180
very hard	10.5 and over	180 and over

You can have a sample of your water tested by a water-conditioning contractor, the Agricultural Extension Service at state universities (or their local branches), the local health department, or by a private testing laboratory. But before you go that far, check for the obvious symptoms of hard water such as whitish, scaly deposits in bathroom fixtures, pots, pans, tea kettles, and coffee makers. You may notice a slow, long-term reduction in your water pressure as mineral deposits build up in water-supply pipes. You may find yourself turning up the thermostat on your water heater as deposits in the bottom of the tank retard heat transfer. But the most obvious sign is a low, curdlike lather when you wash with soap.

If any of these symptoms ring a bell, try this simple test before you call in a water-conditioning contractor. Add ten drops of liquid detergent to a glass of your tap water. Shake it until suds form. Now take a look: if they're high and foamy you have soft water; if the suds form a low curd instead of light bubbles, your water is hard. For a comparison, try the same test on a glass of distilled (pure) water—it's as soft as water can be.

SERVICES

Water-treatment services can be bought or rented; if you rent, include an option to buy in the agreement. The most basic treatment is called soft-water service, which is best suited for moderate hardness where only a moderate amount of water is used. With this service, a portable appliance is connected to your water line and the filter unit is changed periodically.

When the water supply is hard and consumption is increased, treatment is made with a water conditioner that is permanently connected to your plumbing system. It should remove sediment that can clog aerators and screens on faucets, and reduce hardness to 1.0 gpg or less. Small amounts of iron (it leaves orangey-red stains under dripping faucets) will be removed as well.

Another type of appliance, called a chemical feeder, can be attached at your well or water supply to neutralize excessive iron deposits, sulfur (actually hydrogen sulfide gas that gives water a rotten-egg odor and can tarnish silverware), acidic water, or a high bacterial count. It's like a controlled chlorination of a swimming pool. Chemical feeders may be used alone or in conjunction with a softener.

QUALIFICATIONS

To provide effective water conditioning a contractor must be able to evaluate your water supply, select equipment that will improve water quality and remove damaging or health-threatening impurities, and install the equipment as an efficient, integral part of your plumbing system.

The Water Quality Association (WQA) maintains a voluntary certification program for water-conditioning dealers, and another for installers. Applicants for dealer certification are expected to have at least one year of dealership experience, and then must pass a three-hundred-question exam. Installer certification is granted after a general exam on conditioning equipment, plumbing hardware, piping, and layout planning.

A WQA gold seal certification on conditioning equipment (sold by any dealer or contractor) indicates that the equipment meets or exceeds industry standards.

You may get recommendations from a plumbing contractor, but the best sources are several of the installer's former clients. Ask for the names of a few long-term clients so you can check on servicing.

PROFESSIONAL PRACTICES

A prescription for effective water treatment can't be made until a sample of your tap water is tested. Experienced contractors should be able to give you a rough diagnosis on the spot, just from the sight, smell, and taste; they should back it up with a detailed test report.

The contractor should inspect your plumbing system to see how it can accommodate conditioning equipment. Single- or double-tank models can be used, but their capacity should be measured carefully. Undersized units can restrict water flow. To get an accurate estimate, the contractor should inquire about the number of baths and showers taken in the household, and the type and capacity of water-consuming appliances and how frequently they are used. If your water is metered (bought from a water-utility company) your gallon consumption will be on the bill. Lawn-sprinkling systems and outside faucets should not be counted, and should be bypassed by the conditioning system (your lawn doesn't need conditioned water).

A detailed estimate should list all equipment with installation and operating costs (how often the unit must be recharged, with how much salt, and at what cost). The manufacturer's name, type of appliance, capacity, and warranty should be listed plus the location and date of installation.

All water-conditioning contractors are expected to follow local plumbing codes, and it is considered good practice to use the type of piping already in your home to make all connections. This may be difficult in homes with plastic pipe, which can mean extra work and cost to electrically ground the appliance as well. But in any system, either a three-way valve or three separate valves should be installed so you have the option to bypass the conditioning system. Finally, your contractor should warrant the installation to a specific level of performance. If your water is hard (7.9 to 10.5 gpg), you should have a written assurance that it will be 1.0 gpg or less after the job. Similar statements should be made about removing other impurities.

EVALUATING WORK

Softening equipment is required and selected largely on the basis of your water quality, and this makes the results of the contractor's tests crucial. You can verify these findings by having another sample tested at a branch of the Agricultural Extension Service, local health department, or a private lab. If your water is metered, check with the water company. The supply may already be treated to a specific level, even if it is not the level you're looking for.

You can evaluate the contractor's check of your plumbing system and water use in several ways. If you have a private well check with the well driller (they keep a log) and the pump-service company to verify capacity and pressure. If you are on a meter, simply multiply the flow (measured in cubic feet) by 1.1 to estimate the daily consumption in gallons. As a general rule, figure up to 50 gal. a day per family member.

To double check the contractor's recommendations for conditioning capacity, multiply the grains per gallon (gpg) content of the tested sample by the number of gallons consumed daily. The recommended equipment should slightly exceed this capacity.

Always call the health department in addition to several water-conditioning contractors if there is a potential health problem—if, for example, there is a high bacteria count in your well water because of seepage from a nearby septic system. Their recommendations can be compared to the contractor's proposal.

GRIEVANCES

Complaints about WQA-certified dealers or installers should be directed to the Water Quality Association (WQA, 477 East Butterfield Rd., Lombard, IL 60148). If contractual or financial problems arise with any dealer or contractor, follow the general grievance procedures outlined in the Primer.

If you feel that the conditioning system is adversely affecting your health, consult a physician, call in the health department, and recall the conditioning contractor. People on strictly controlled diets, particularly low-sodium diets, may wish to check any major change in the chemical composition of their water with their physician.

Well Drillers

In some areas of Long Island, bottled-water companies are doing a booming business—a lot of homeowners are drinking it because the water coming out of their taps is hazardous to their health.

Try to imagine your household without a convenient, constant source of clean water. It could happen no matter where you live. In metropolitan areas, you may have to depend on government agencies that have mismanaged watersheds and failed to cross-connect storage systems so that some reservoirs dry up while others overflow. That's exactly what happened in northern New Jersey during the 1981 drought. In suburban areas the water company may not always have the amount of water you're willing to pay for, even when they tack premiums onto regular rates, like a flat $500 fee for filling a swimming pool. In rural areas, 80 percent of the households have to depend on their own well water.

A supply of potable water is essential in any household. And if the water company doesn't bring it to the door where you live, you have to call someone in to dig for it. Now the odds of striking water are a lot better than striking oil, but like an oil well, a water well can deteriorate and run dry.

If you buy land or a house that needs a well, a driller has to start from scratch by surveying the terrain for a well site that is likely to produce water. About 85 percent of drilled wells are successful. The rest become magnificent gopher holes. If you're looking at a house that already has a well, consider carefully its location, size, construction, and capacity as part of your over-all home inspection before buying.

SERVICES

A well driller should be able to conduct an evaluation of the terrain based on established geologic principles to determine where he will find quality water. As drillers charge by the foot drilled, this is an extremely important part of the project. There's nothing quite so depressing as a 200-ft. dry hole at $15 a foot. And there's nothing to do if you get one but start another hole.

When a site is chosen, the driller will generally bring in a portable derrick—a $100,000-plus piece of machinery that takes well drilling well out of the ballpark for fly-by-nighters. Test holes may be bored if surface indications of water are unclear or altogether absent. This produces rock samples that can be tested for moisture content. Test holes cost a lot less than well holes, and can be a reasonable way to hedge your 85 percent drilling bet if the initial indicators are not promising.

Almost 90 percent of all groundwater is in the top 200 ft., and the average depth of domestic wells in this country is less than 50 ft. But each site is different. A contractor may use a system called cable-tool drilling, where a chisel-shaped weight crushes rock in the hole, or rotary drilling, where a cutting bit backed by sections of hollow rod is used. Well drillers should be able to line this bored hole, install a pump matched to the capacity of the well and the demands of your household, and provide a sanitary seal that prevents contamination from surface impurities.

They should also be well informed about local sanitary codes that restrict well location in relation to the house structure and any septic systems in the area. In some states, you are required to file a Statement of Intent to drill, and conduct a coliform potability test (this counts bacteria in the water) before a Certificate of Approval is granted by the health department.

QUALIFICATIONS

The National Well Water Association (NWWA) conducts a certification program that requires at least two years' experience in an operational or supervisory capacity for applicants in their well-drilling or pump-installation programs. In many states, a license is required for well drillers (call your building or health department to check), which the NWWA requires before it grants certification.

The NWWA program includes general and specialty exams, and if applicants pass exams in two or more categories, with scores of 90 percent or better (and have at least five years of professional experience), they may be granted one of two titles: Certified Well Driller (CWD), or Certified Pump Installer (CPI).

A solid knowledge of the local terrain is very important—it greatly increases the chance of hitting quality water the first time around. A local company with a long record of success will have many drilling logs, which include detailed records of the type and composition of different strata encountered as each one of their wells was drilled.

Recommendations, in addition to those of the driller's past clients, may be obtained from a local county agricultural agent, local health department officers who regularly inspect wells, from pump and well-equipment dealers, and from the NWWA directory.

PROFESSIONAL PRACTICES

No driller can guarantee the amount of water a well will produce or its quality. Looking for water is nitty-gritty detective work, and short-cuts can lead to the wrong conclusions. It's surprising, though, how many homeowners pay for a completely unscientific answer by hiring a dowser. They're also called water witches, and most of them use a forked stick, some other kind of divining rod, or simply the sensations they say come through their fingertips, to sense the presence of water underground.

Now I'm always ready for new ways to get results, but there's no way I'll recommend that you consult a dowser, even though this is probably the one field in this book where recommendations carry the most weight. I know several homeowners who recommend the dowser they hired the way they would recommend a faith healer who restored their sight. And that's a powerful, personal recommendation. You can't argue with success, even if it was an accident. But I know a dowser who has found many water sources, a buried existing well, even the location of an old septic tank that had been covered with several feet of soil for about fifteen years. Don't laugh. Dowsers even have their own professional society, and many of the members have a rate of success that defies the laws of probability.

Professional well drillers, on the other hand, have a somewhat more reliable way of doing business. Most of them begin with an appraisal of the terrain, an expert opinion for which there is a fee, usually charged by the hour. All or most of it should be applied to drilling costs if the appraising contractor digs your well within a year.

Before he starts, you should negotiate a contract that includes the driller's license, names and addresses of all parties, a description of the property, and the specific well site (25 ft. south of the southwest corner of the house, 18 ft. east of the driveway, for example). Particulars about the well should include the drilling method, estimated depth of the finished well, the casing material and length, the type and specifications of the sanitary seal, the drilling cost per foot, casing cost per foot, and all material, equipment, and labor charges for tests, pumps, piping, and hardware required to produce an approved, pumping well. A certified well log, sometimes called a driller's report, should be delivered to you when the job is done.

Be sure the driller specifies that all work will conform to local codes. Generally, wells must be located higher than the septic system or other drainage systems. And minimum distances between the well and structures or drainage systems must be observed.

The driller should select a pump according to the well depth and diameter, which may be different at the pumping level and at ground level. A separate, code-approved electrical circuit must be provided.

Well capacity can't be accurately predicted before the well is drilled. You'll probably need about 50 gal. per day per member of the household. But even a low-yielding well, providing only 1 gal. per minute, may be sufficient for a family of four requiring 200 gal. a day if a storage tank is installed. There are 1,440 minutes in a day, enough time for a 1 gal.-per-minute well to pump the same number of gallons. The common productivity rate is 4 to 10 gpm.

EVALUATING WORK

The age of a local business practice is about the best indicator of quality, assuming the contractor has no black marks for abnormal business practices. It's hard to stay in business with a record of one dry hole after another, right? An NWWA affiliation and expert certification help. But you can verify some of the information and recommendations a driller supplies by contacting the nearest branch of the U.S. Geological Survey. Write their headquarters (USGS Water Resources Div., 12201 Sunrise Valley Dr., Reston, VA 22092) for information on local water resources and conditions, and the address of the branch nearest you. This information is free.

You can also double-check some of the driller's water-locating methods. In addition to well logs, experienced drillers check the landscape carefully for trees and plants that thrive only in areas where their roots reach the water table. They are called phreatophytes. In arid regions, they may be the best indicator. Willow and cottonwood trees, for example, generally indicate good water 20 ft. down. Check the Agricultural Extension Service in your area or write for a copy of "Guide for Surveying Phreatophyte Vegetation" (publication AH 266) from the U.S. Department of Agriculture (USDA, Office of Information, Washington, DC 20250).

Drillers want to bring in a wet well. Dry ones don't get them recommendations. But if you are one of the unfortunate 15 percent that do come up empty, ask for an explanation. Sometimes a cavity can be caused in the water table, called a cone of depression, by demands of neighboring wells. Your driller should check thoroughly into local use of the water table.

GRIEVANCES

For affiliated and certified members, direct grievances to the National Water Well Association (NWWA, 500 W. Wilson Bridge Rd., Worthington, OH 43085). For complaints about business practices follow the general grievance procedures in the Primer.

Health or sanitary problems should be directed to the local health department. In most areas, they are prepared to take a tap-water sample and conduct a free coliform potability test to see if your well is contaminated. If the bacteria count is above minimal levels, they may conduct a dye test to track septic overflows or seepage from your or your neighbor's septic systems.

APPENDIX:

CONSUMER INFORMATION SOURCES

Regional Offices of Key Federal Consumer Agencies

The federal government is not in the business of recommending a local plumber. But it does spend some of your tax dollars on home-related research and testing, setting up information services, loan programs, and many other activities that can help you.

Regional offices of the most pertinent federal agencies are listed here. If you contact them, I suggest the following guidelines:

1. Be specific, use recognizable terminology, ask for literature by title and number. General questions will receive general answers.

2. Always ask for names, titles, addresses, and phone numbers of personnel who will be able to help you if the person you reach (by letter or phone) cannot.

3. Allow enough time for two round-trip letters. Frequently, the response to your first letter, no matter how clear and concise you make it, will net only a list of available documents or addresses of related programs and agencies from which you can pick the right source that can really help.

CONSUMER PRODUCT SAFETY COMMISSION

Atlanta 1330 W. Peachtree St. NW, Atlanta, GA 30309, (404) 881-2231

Boston 100 Summer St., Room 1607, Boston, MA 02110, (617) 223-5576

Chicago 230 S. Dearborn St., Room 2945, Chicago, IL 60604, (312) 353-8260

Cleveland Plaza 9 Bldg., Suite 520, 55 Erieview Plaza, Cleveland, OH 44114, (216) 522-3886

Dallas 500 S. Ervay, Room 410C, Dallas, TX 75201, (214) 749-3871

Denver Guaranty Bank Bldg., 817 17th St., Suite 938, Denver, CO 80202, (303) 837-2904

Kansas City Traders National Bank Bldg., 1125 Grand Ave., Suite 1500, Kansas City, MO 64106, (816) 374-2034

Los Angeles 3660 Wilshire Blvd., Suite 1100, Los Angeles, CA 90010, (213) 688-7272

New York 6 World Trade Center, Vesey St., 6th floor, New York, NY 10048, (212) 264-1125

Philadelphia 400 Market St., 10th floor, Philadelphia, PA 19106, (215) 597-9105

St. Paul Metro Square, 7th & Robert, Suite 580, St. Paul, MN 55101, (612) 725-7781

San Francisco 100 Pine St., Suite 500, San Francisco, CA 94111, (415) 556-1816

Seattle 3240 Federal Bldg., 915 Second Ave., Seattle, WA 98174, (206) 442-5276

DEPARTMENT OF ENERGY

Atlanta 1655 Peachtree St. NE, 8th floor, Atlanta, GA 30309, (404) 881-2838

Boston Analex Bldg., 150 Causeway St., Room 700, Boston, MA 02114, (617) 223-3701

Chicago 175 W. Jackson Blvd., Room A333, Chicago, IL 60604, (312) 353-0540

Dallas PO Box 35228, 2626 W. Mockingbird Ln., Dallas, TX 75235, (214) 749-7345

Kansas City 324 E. 11th St., Kansas City, MO 64106, (816) 374-2061

Lakewood PO Box 26247—Belmar Branch, 1075 S. Yukon St., Lakewood, CO 80226, (303) 234-2420

New York 26 Federal Plaza, Room 3206, New York, NY 10007, (212) 264-1021

Philadelphia 1421 Cherry St., 10th floor, Philadelphia, PA 19102, (215) 597-3890

San Francisco 111 Pine St., 3rd floor, San Francisco, CA 94111, (415) 556-7216

Seattle 1992 Federal Bldg., 915 Second Ave., Seattle, WA 98174, (206) 442-7280

DEPARTMENT OF HEALTH, EDUCATION AND WELFARE

Atlanta 50 7th St. NE, Atlanta, GA 30323, (404) 221-2442

Boston John F. Kennedy Federal Bldg., Boston, MA 02203, (617) 223-6831

Chicago 300 S. Wacker Dr., Chicago, IL 60606, (312) 353-5160
Dallas 1200 Main Tower Bldg., Dallas, TX 75202, (214) 655-3301
Denver 1961 Stout St., Denver, CO 80202, (303) 837-3373
Kansas City 601 E. 12th. St., Kansas City, MO 64106, (816) 374-3436
New York 26 Federal Plaza, New York, NY 10007, (212) 264-4600
Philadelphia 3535 Market St., Philadelphia, PA 19101, (215) 596-6492
San Francisco 50 Fulton St., San Francisco, CA 94102, (415) 556-6746
Seattle 1321 Second Ave., Seattle, WA 98101, (206) 442-0420

DEPARTMENT OF HOUSING AND URBAN DEVELOPMENT

Atlanta Pershing Point Plaza, 1371 Peachtree St. NW, Atlanta, GA 30309, (404) 881-4585
Boston John F. Kennedy Federal Bldg., Room 800, Boston, MA 02203, (617) 223-4066
Chicago 300 S. Wacker Dr., Chicago, IL 60606, (312) 353-5680
Dallas Earl Cabell Federal Bldg., 1100 Commerce St., Dallas, TX 75242, (214) 749-7401
Denver Executive Towers, 1405 Curtis St., Denver, CO 80202, (303) 837-4513
Kansas City 300 Federal Office Bldg., 911 Walnut St., Kansas City, MO 64106, (816) 374-2661
New York 25 Federal Plaza, New York, NY 10007, (212) 264-8068
Philadelphia Curtis Bldg., 6th & Walnut Sts., Philadelphia, PA 19106, (215) 597-2560
San Francisco 450 Golden Gate Ave., PO Box 36003, San Francisco, CA 94102, (415) 556-4752
Seattle 3003 Arcade Plaza Bldg., 1321 Second Ave., Seattle, WA 98101, (206) 442-5414

ENVIRONMENTAL PROTECTION AGENCY

Atlanta 345 Courtland St. NE, Atlanta, GA 30308, (404) 881-4727
Boston John F. Kennedy Federal Bldg., Boston, MA 02203, (617) 223-7210
Chicago 230 S. Dearborn St., Chicago, IL 60604, (312) 353-2000
Dallas 1201 Elm St., Dallas, TX 75270, (214) 767-2600
Denver 1860 Lincoln St., Denver, CO 80203, (303) 837-3895
Kansas City 324 E. 11th St., Kansas City, MO 64106, (816) 374-5493

New York 26 Federal Plaza, New York, NY 10007, (212) 264-2525
Philadelphia 6th & Walnut Sts., Philadelphia, PA 19106, (215) 597-9814
San Francisco 215 Fremont St., San Francisco, CA 94105, (415) 556-2320
Seattle 1200 Sixth Ave., Seattle, WA 98101, (206) 442-1220

FEDERAL TRADE COMMISSION

Atlanta 1718 Peachtree St. NW, Room 1000, Atlanta, GA 30309, (404) 881-4836
Boston 150 Causeway St., Room 1301, Boston, MA 02114, (617) 223-6621
Chicago 55 E. Monroe St., Suite 1437, Chicago, IL 60603, (312) 353-4423
Cleveland Mall Bldg., 118 St. Clair Ave., Suite 500, Cleveland, OH 44144, (216) 522-4207
Dallas 2001 Bryan St., Suite 2665, Dallas, TX 75201, (214) 729-0032
Denver 1405 Curtis St., Suite 2900, Denver, CO 80202 (303) 837-2271
Los Angeles Federal Bldg., 11000 Wilshire Blvd., Room 13209, Los Angeles, CA 90024, (213) 824-7575
New York Federal Bldg., 26 Federal Plaza, Room 2243-EB, New York NY 10007, (212) 264-1207
San Francisco 450 Golden Gate Ave., Box 36005, San Francisco, CA 94102, (415) 556-1270
Seattle Federal Bldg., 915 Second Ave., 28th floor, Seattle, WA 98174, (206) 442-4655

FOREST SERVICE

Albuquerque Federal Bldg., 517 Gold Ave. SW, Albuquerque, NM 87102, (505) 766-2401
Atlanta 1720 Peachtree Rd. NW, Atlanta, GA 30309, (404) 881-4177
Juneau Federal Office Bldg., PO Box 1628, Juneau, AK 99802, (907) 586-7263
Lakewood 11177 W. 8th Ave., Box 25127, Lakewood, CO 80225, (303) 234-3711
Milwaukee 633 W. Wisconsin Ave., Milwaukee, WI 53203, (414) 224-3693
Missoula Federal Bldg., Missoula, MT 59807, (406) 329-3011

Ogden 324 25th St., Ogden, UT 84401, (801) 399-6011

Portland 319 SW Pine St., PO Box 3623, Portland, OR 97208, (503) 221-3625

San Francisco 630 Sansome St., San Francisco, CA 94111, (415) 556-4318

OCCUPATIONAL SAFETY AND HEALTH ADMINISTRATION

Atlanta 1375 Peachtree St. NE, Suite 587, Atlanta, GA 30309, (404) 881-3573

Boston John F. Kennedy Federal Bldg., Room 1804, Boston, MA 02203, (617) 223-6712

Chicago 230 S. Dearborn St., 32nd floor, Chicago, IL 60604, (312) 353-2220

Dallas 555 Griffin Sq., Room 602, Dallas, TX 75202, (214) 767-4731

Denver Federal Bldg., 1961 Stout St., Room 1554, Denver, CO 80294, (303) 837-3883

Kansas City 911 Walnut St., Room 3000, Kansas City, MO 64106, (816) 374-5861

New York 1 Astor Plaza, 1515 Broadway, Room 3445, New York, NY 10036, (212) 399-5754

Philadelphia Gateway Bldg., 3535 Market St., Suite 2100, Philadelphia, PA 19104, (215) 596-1201

San Francisco Box 36017, 450 Golden Gate Ave., San Francisco, CA 94102, (415) 556-0586

Seattle Federal Office Bldg., 909 First Ave., Room 6048, Seattle, WA 98174, (206) 442-5930

State, County, and City Consumer Offices

This listing has four different kinds of consumer agencies: (1) state consumer headquarters and, in some states, their local branches; (2) county consumer offices; (3) city consumer agencies in and around metropolitan areas; and (4) specialized state agencies that handle questions on banking and financing, energy use, and utility companies.

As a rule of thumb, remember that larger agencies which cover more territory and more people will tend to give you state guidelines and policies—the big picture. Local agencies that are familiar with local building codes, housing characteristics, financing practices, even the contractor you're inquiring about, are more likely to provide practical help.

ALABAMA

Governor's Office of Consumer Protection, 138 Adams Ave., Montgomery, AL 36130, (205) 832-5936, (800-392-5658)
Consumer Services Director, Office of Attorney General, 669 S. Lawrence St., Montgomery, AL 36104, (205) 834-5150

Banking: Superintendent of Banks, 651 Administration Bldg., Montgomery AL 36130
Energy: Alabama Energy Management Board, Montgomery, AL 36130, (205) 832-5010
Utilities: Alabama Public Service Commission, PO Box 991, Montgomery, AL 36130, (205) 832-3421

ALASKA

Consumer Protection Section, Office of Attorney General, 420 L St., Suite 100, Anchorage, AK 99501, (907) 279-0428. *Branch Office:* State Court Office Bldg., Room 228, Fairbanks, AK 99707, (907) 465-3692. *Branch Office:* Pouch K, Room 1568, State Capitol, Juneau, AK 99811, (907) 465-3692

Banking: Director of Banking and Securities, Pouch D, Juneau, AK 99811, (907) 465-2521

Energy: State Energy Office, MacKay Bldg., 338 Denali St., Anchorage, AK 99501, (907) 272-0508

Utilities: Alaska Public Utilities Commission, 1100 MacKay Bldg., 338 Denali St., Anchorage, AK 99501, (907) 276-6222

ARIZONA

Financial Fraud Office, 207 State Capitol Bldg., Phoenix, AZ 85007, (602) 255-5763. *Branch Office:* Economic Protection Division, 100 N. Stone Ave., Suite 1004, Tucson, AZ 85701, (602) 882-5501

Cochise County Chief Investigator, Cochise County Attorney's Office, PO Drawer CA, Bisbee, AZ 85603, (602) 432-5703

Pima County Consumer Protection/Economic Crime Unit, Pima County Attorney's Office, 111 W. Congress, Tucson, AZ 85701, (602) 792-8668

Yuma County Yuma County Attorney's Office, PO Box 1048, Yuma, AZ 85364, (602) 782-4534, ext. 55

Phoenix Mayor's Citizens Assistance Office, 251 W. Washington, Phoenix, AZ 85003, (602) 262-7777

Tucson Public Affairs Division, Tucson City Attorney's Office, PO Box 27210, Tucson, AZ 85726, (602) 791-4886

Banking: Superintendent of Banks, 101 Commerce Bldg., 1601 W. Jefferson St., Phoenix, AZ 85007, (602) 255-4421

Energy: Energy Office, Office of Economic Planning and Development, 507 Capitol Tower, Phoenix, AZ 85007, (602) 255-3632

ARKANSAS

Consumer Protection Division, Attorney General's Office, Justice Bldg., Little Rock, AR 72201, (501) 371-2341 (800-482-8982)

Banking: State Bank Commissioner, 1 Capitol Mall, 4-B 210, Little Rock, AR 72201, (501) 371-1117

Energy: Dept. of Energy, 3000 Kavanaugh Blvd., Little Rock, AR 72205, (501) 371-1370

Utilities: Arkansas Public Service Commission, 400 Union Sta., Little Rock, AR 72201, (501) 371-1451

CALIFORNIA

California Dept. of Consumer Affairs, 1020 N St., Sacramento, CA 95814, (916) 445-0660 (complaint mediation); (916) 445-1254 (consumer information). *Branch Office:* 107 S. Broadway, Room 8020, Los Angeles, CA 90012, (213) 620-4360. *Branch Office:* 30 Van Ness Ave., Room 2100, San Francisco, CA 94102, (415) 557-2046. *Branch Office:* Public Inquiry Unit, Office of Attorney General, 555 Capitol Mall, Sacramento, CA 95814, (916) 322-3360

Alameda County Deputy District Attorney, 24405 Amador St., Hayward, CA 94544, (415) 881-6150

Contra Costa County Special Operations Div., District Attorney's Office, PO Box 670, 725 Court St., Martinez, CA 94553, (415) 372-4500

Del Norte County Div. of Consumer Affairs, 2650 Washington Blvd., Crescent City, CA 95531, (707) 464-2716 or 3756

Fresno County Dept. of Weights, Measures, and Consumer Protection, 4535 E. Hamilton Ave., Fresno, CA 93702, (209) 453-5904 Consumer Fraud Div., District Attorney's Office, Courthouse, 1100 Van Ness Ave., Fresno, CA 93721, (209) 488-3141

Kern County Deputy District Attorney, Consumer Unit, 1415 Truxton Ave., Bakersfield, CA 93301, (805) 861-2421

Los Angeles County Consumer and Environmental Protection Div., District Attorney's Office, 320 W. Temple, Los Angeles, CA 90012, (213) 974-3970 Dept. of Consumer Affairs, 500 W. Temple St., Room B-96, Los Angeles, CA 90012, (213) 974-1452

Madera County Consumer Protection Unit, Madera County Weights and Measures, 902 N. Gateway Dr., Madera, CA 93637, (209) 674-4641

Mendocino County Deputy District Attorney, Consumer Unit, PO Box 1000, Ukiah, CA 95482, (707) 468-4211

Napa County Deputy District Attorney, Consumer Affairs Div., 1125 3rd St., Napa, CA 94558, (707) 253-4427

Orange County Office of Consumer Affairs, 511 N. Sycamore St., Santa Ana, CA 92701, (714) 834-6100

Major Fraud and Economic Crime Unit, District Attorney's Office, 700 Civic Center Dr. W., Santa Ana, CA 92702, (714) 834-3600

Riverside County Deputy District Attorney, Economic Crime Div., PO Box 1148, Riverside, CA 92502, (714) 787-6372

Sacramento County Consumer Protection Bureau, 827 7th St., Room 43, Sacramento, CA 95814, (916) 440-5893
District Attorney's Fraud Div., PO Box 749, Sacramento, CA 95804, (916) 440-6823

San Diego County Consumer Fraud Div., District Attorney's Office, PO Box X-1011, San Diego, CA 92112, (714) 236-2474

San Francisco County Consumer Fraud Economic Crime Unit, District Attorney's Office, 880 Bryant St., Room 320, San Francisco, CA 94103, (415) 553-1821

San Joaquin County Deputy District Attorney, PO Box 50, Stockton, CA 95201, (209) 944-2411

San Luis Obispo County Consumer Unit, District Attorney's Office, 302 Courthouse Annex, San Luis Obispo, CA 93408, (805) 549-5800

San Mateo County Deputy District Attorney, Hall of Justice and Records, Redwood City, CA 94063, (415) 364-5600

Santa Barbara County Consumer Business Law Section, 118 E. Figeroa, Santa Barbara, CA 93101, (805) 963-1441

Santa Clara County Dept. of Consumer Affairs, 1555 Berger Dr., San Jose, CA 95112, (408) 299-4211
Consumer Fraud Unit, District Attorney's Office, 70 W. Hedding St., West Wing, San Jose, CA 95110, (408) 275-9651

Santa Cruz County Div. of Consumer Affairs, County Bldg., 701 Ocean St., Room 240, Santa Cruz, CA 95060, (408) 425-2054
Consumer Protection Unit, District Attorney's Office, PO Box 1159, Santa Cruz, CA 95061, (408) 425-2071

Solano County Consumer Fraud Unit, District Attorney's Office, 600 Union Ave., Fairfield, CA 94533, (707) 429-6451

Stanislaus County Office of Consumer Affairs, 921 County Center No. 3 Ct., Room 60, Modesto, CA 95355, (209) 526-6211
Consumer Fraud Unit, District Attorney's Office, PO Box 442, Modesto, CA 95353, (209) 577-0570

Sutter County Office of Consumer Affairs, Dept. of Weights and Measures, 142 Garden Highway, Yuba City, CA 95991, (916) 674-2851

Ventura County   Consumer Fraud Section, District Attorney's Office, 800 S. Victoria Ave., Ventura, CA 93009, (805) 654-3110
Consumer Fraud Economic Crime Unit, District Attorney's Office, 800 S. Victoria Ave., Ventura, CA 93009, (805) 654-3110
Yolo County   Consumer Fraud Div., District Attorney's Office, PO Box 412, Woodland, CA 95695, (916) 666-8521

Los Angeles   Consumer Protection Section, City Attorney's Office, 200 N. Main St., Los Angeles, CA 90012, (213) 485-4515
San Diego   Consumer Protection Unit, City Attorney's Office, 1200 Third Ave., San Diego, CA 92101, (714) 236-6007
Santa Monica   Consumer Division, City Attorney's Office, 1685 Main St., Santa Monica, CA 90401, (213) 393-9975

Banking: Superintendent of Banks, 235 Montgomery St., Suite 750, San Francisco, CA 94104, (415) 557-3535
Energy: California Energy Commission, 1111 Howe Ave., Sacramento, CA 95825, (916) 920-6811 (800-852-7516)
Utilities: California Public Utilities Commission, California State Bldg., 350 McAllister St., San Francisco, CA 94102, (415) 557-1487

COLORADO

Consumer Section, 1525 Sherman St., 4th floor, Denver, CO 80203, (303) 839-3611
Uniform Consumer Credit Code, Office of Attorney General, 1525 Sherman St., Denver, CO 80203, (303) 839-3611

Archuleta, LaPlata, and San Juan Counties   District Attorney's Office, PO Box 1062, Durango, CO 81301, (303) 247-8850
Adams, Arapahoe, Denver, and Jefferson Counties   Metro District Attorney's Consumer Office, 625 S. Broadway, Denver, CO 80209, (303) 777-3072
Boulder County   District Attorney's Consumer Office, PO Box 471, Boulder, CO 80306, (303) 441-3700
El Paso and Teller Counties   District Attorney's Consumer Office, 27 E. Vermijo, Suite 413, County Office Bldg., Colorado Springs, CO 80903, (303) 471-5861
Larimer County   District Attorney's Consumer Office, Rocky Mountain Bank Bldg., PO Box 1969, Ft. Collins, CO 80522, (303) 221-2100, ext. 460

Pueblo County District Attorney's Consumer Office, Courthouse, 10th and Main Sts., Pueblo, CO 81003, (303) 543-3550
Weld County District Attorney's Consumer Office, PO Box 1167, Greeley, CO 80632, (303) 356-4000

Banking: State Bank Commissioner, 325 State Office Bldg., Denver, CO 80203, (303) 839-3131
Energy: State Energy Office, 1600 Downing, 2nd floor, Denver, CO 80218, (303) 839-2507
Utilities: Colorado Public Utilities Commission, 500 State Services Bldg., 1525 Sherman St., Denver, CO 80203, (303) 839-3154

CONNECTICUT

Department of Consumer Protection, State Office Bldg., Hartford, CT 06115, (203) 566-4999 (800-842-2649)
Office of Consumer Protection, City Hall, Middletown, CT 06457, (203) 347-4671

Banking: Bank Commissioner, 239 State Office Bldg., 165 Capitol Ave., Hartford, CT 06115, (203) 566-7580
Energy: Energy Div., Office of Policy and Management, 80 Washington St., Hartford, CT 06115, (203) 566-2800
Utilities: Div. of Consumer Counsel, Dept. of Business Regulation, 545 State Office Bldg., Hartford, CT 06115, (203) 566-7287

DELAWARE

Consumer Affairs Div., Dept. of Community Affairs and Economic Development, 820 N. French St., Wilmington, DE 19801, (302) 571-3250
Dept. of Justice, 820 N. French St., Wilmington, DE 19801, (302) 571-2500

Energy: Governor's Energy Office, 114 W. Water St., PO Box 1401, Dover, DE 19901, (302) 678-5644
Utilities: Office of Public Advocate, Dept. of Community Affairs and Economic Development, 820 N. French St., Wilmington, DE 19801, (302) 571-3250

DISTRICT OF COLUMBIA

D.C. Office of Consumer Protection, 1424 K St. NW, Washington, DC 20005, (202) 727-1158

Energy: D.C. Energy Unit, Jackson School, 31st & R Sts. NW, Washington, DC 20007, (202) 727-1800
Utilities: D.C. Public Service Commission, Cafritz Bldg., 1625 I St. NW, Room 204, Washington, DC 20006, (202) 727-3050

FLORIDA

Div. of Consumer Services, 110 Mayo Bldg., Tallahassee, FL 32304, (904) 488-2221 (800-342-2176)
Consumer Protection and Fair Trade Practices Bureau, Dept. of Legal Affairs, State Capitol, Tallahassee, FL 32304, (904) 488-8916. *Branch Office:* Dade County Regional Service Center, 401 NW 2nd Ave., Suite 820, Miami, FL 33128, (305) 377-5441. *Branch Office:* Asst. Attorney General, 1313 Tampa St. Park Trammell, Tampa, FL 33602, (813) 272-2670
Office of Public Counsel, 4 Holland Bldg., Tallahassee, FL 32304, (904) 488-9330 (litigation only)
Dept. of Business Regulation, The Johns Bldg., Tallahassee, FL 32304, (904) 488-9820

Brevard County Consumer Fraud Div., State Attorney's Office, County Courthouse, Titusville, FL 32780, (305) 269-8401
Broward County Consumer Affairs Div., 236 SE 1st Ave., Fort Lauderdale, FL 33301, (305) 765-5306
Dade County Consumer Protection Div., Metro Dade County, 140 W. Flagler St., Miami, FL 33130, (305) 579-4222
South Dade Government Center, 10710 SW 211th St., Miami, FL 33189, (305) 232-1810
Consumer Fraud Div., Office of State Attorney, 1351 NW 12th St., Miami, FL 33125, (305) 547-5200
Consumer Advocate, Metropolitan Dade County, 140 W. Flagler St., Miami, FL 33130, (305) 579-4206
Desoto, Manatee, and Sarasota Counties Office of State Attorney, 2070 Main St., Sarasota, FL 33577, (813) 955-0918
Duval County Div. of Consumer Affairs, Dept. of Human Resources, 614 City Hall, Jacksonville, FL 32202, (904) 633-3429

Hillsborough County   Hillsborough Co. Dept. of Consumer Affairs, 3725 Grace St., Tampa, FL 33607, (813) 272-6750
Palm Beach County   Dept. of Consumer Affairs, 301 N. Olive Ave., West Palm Beach, FL 33401, (305) 837-2670
Economic Crime Unit, Office of State Attorney, PO Drawer 2905, West Palm Beach, FL 33402, (305) 837-2239
Pinellas County   Office of Consumer Affairs, Office of State Attorney, 801 W. Bay Drive, Suite 610, Largo, FL 33540, (813) 448-3801
Seminole County   Consumer Fraud Div., Office of State Attorney, 149 Seminole County Courthouse, Stanford, FL 32771, (305) 322-7534

Lauderhill   Consumer Affairs Committee, 1080 NW 47th Ave., Lauderhill, FL 33313, (305) 584-9521
Tamarac   Board of Consumer Affairs, City of Tamarac, 5811 NW 88th Ave., Tamarac, FL 33321, (305) 722-5900

Banking: Comptroller of Florida, State Capitol Bldg., Tallahassee, FL 32304, (904) 488-0370
Energy: State Energy Office, 108 Collins Bldg., Tallahassee, FL 32304, (904) 488-6764
Utilities: Office of Consumer Affairs, Public Service Commission, Fletcher Bldg., Tallahassee, FL 32304, (904) 488-7238 (800-342-3552)

GEORGIA

Governor's Office of Consumer Affairs, 225 Peachtree St. NE, Suite 400, Atlanta, GA 30303, (404) 656-4900 (800-282-4900)
Deceptive Practices Div., Office of Attorney General, 132 State Judicial Bldg., Atlanta, GA 30334, (404) 656-3391

Atlanta   Office of Consumer Affairs, City Hall, Memorial Drive Annex, 121 Memorial Drive SW, Atlanta, GA 30303, (404) 658-6704

Banking: Commissioner of Banking and Finance, 148 International Blvd. NE, Suite 640, Atlanta, GA 30303, (404) 656-2050
Energy: Office of Energy Resources, Office of Planning and Budget, 270 Washington St. SW, Atlanta, GA 30334, (404) 656-3874
Utilities: Consumer's Utility Counsel, 15 Peachtree St., Suite 933 Atlanta GA 30303, (404) 656-3982

HAWAII

Director of Consumer Protection, Office of the Governor, 250 S. King St., PO Box 3767, Honolulu, HA 96811, 800-548-2560 (administrative and legal office), 800-548-2540 (complaints)

Banking: Director of Regulatory Agencies, PO Box 541, Honolulu, HA 96809, (808) 548-7505
Energy: Dept. of Planning and Economic Development, PO Box 2359, Honolulu, HA 96804
Utilities: Hawaii Public Service Commission, 1164 Bishop St., Suite 911, Honolulu, HA 96813, (808) 548-3990

IDAHO

Consumer Protection Div., Attorney General's Office, State Capitol, Boise, ID 83720, (208) 384-2400 (800-632-5937)

Banking: Director of Finance, State House, Boise, ID 83720, (208) 384-3313
Energy: Office of Energy, State House, Boise, ID 83720, (208) 384-3258
Utilities: Idaho Public Utilities Commission, State House, Boise, ID 83720, (208) 384-3143

ILLINOIS

Consumer Advocate Office, Office of the Governor, 160 N. LaSalle St., Room 2010, Chicago, IL 60601, (312) 793-2754
Consumer Fraud Section, Office of Attorney General, 228 N. LaSalle St., Room 1242, Chicago, IL 60601, (312) 793-3580.
Branch Offices: (write Assistant to the Attorney General for Consumer Affairs at the appropriate address)
2151 Madison, Bellwood, IL 60104, (312) 344-7700
50 Raupp Blvd., Buffalo Grove, IL 60090, (312) 459-2500 (Saturday only)
1104 N. Ashland Ave., Chicago, IL 60622, (312) 793-5638
13051 Grainwood Ave., Blue Island, IL 60406, (312) 597-5531
4750 N. Broadway, Room 216, Chicago, IL 60640, (312) 769-3742
800 Lee St., Des Plaines, IL 60016, (312) 824-4200 (Saturday only)

Evanston Library, 1703 Orrington, Evanston, IL 60204, (312) 866-0300

PO Box 752, 71 N. Ottawa St., Joliet, IL 60434, (815) 727-3019

6250 N. Lincoln Ave., Morton Grove, IL 60050, (312) 965-5030 (Saturday only)

500 Main St., Peoria, IL 61602, (309) 671-3191

301 Rockriver Savings Bldg., Rockford, IL 61101, (815) 968-1881

208 18th St., Rock Island, IL 61201, (309) 786-3303

1000 Schaumberg Road, Schaumberg, IL 60172, (312) 884-7710

5172 Oakton St., Skokie, IL 60077, (312) 674-2522

500 S. 2nd St., Springfield, IL 62706, (217) 782-9011

818 Martin Luther King Dr., St. Louis, IL 62201, (618) 874-2238

163 Lakehurst, Waukegan, IL 60085, (312) 473-3302 (Saturday)

Cook County   Consumer Complaint Div., State's Attorney Office, 303 Daley Ctr., Chicago, IL 60602, (312) 443-8425

Madison County   Office of State's Attorney, 103 Purcell St., Edwardsville, IL 62025, (618) 692-4550

Rock Island County   Illinois State Attorney General, Safety Bldg., Rock Island, IL 61201, (309) 788-7623

Banking: Commissioner of Banks and Trust Companies, 400 Reisch Bldg., 4 W. Capitol Square, Springfield, IL 62701, (217) 782-7966

Energy: Institute of Natural Resources, 309 W. Washington St., Chicago, IL 60606, (312) 793-3870

Utilities: Illinois Commerce Commission, 527 E. Capitol Ave., Springfield, IL 62706, (217) 782-7295

INDIANA

Consumer Protection Div., Office of Attorney General, 215 State House, Indianapolis, IN 46204, (317) 633-6496 (800-382-5516)

Lake County   Prosecuting Attorney, 2293 N. Main St., Crown Point, IN 46307, (219) 738-9055

Marion County   Prosecuting Attorney, 560 City-County Bldg., Indianapolis, IN 46204, (317) 633-3522

Banking: Dept. of Financial Institutions, 1024 State Office Bldg., Indianapolis, IN 46204, (317) 633-4365

Energy: Indiana Energy Group, 440 N. Meridian St., Indianapolis, IN 46204, (317) 232-8940
Utilities: Office of Public Counselor, 807 State Office Bldg., Indianapolis, IN 46204, (317) 633-4659

IOWA

Consumer Protection Div., Office of Attorney General, 1300 E. Walnut, Des Moines, IA 50319, (515) 281-5926
Citizen's Aid Ombudsman, 515 E. 12th St., Des Moines, IA 50319, (515) 281-3592

Banking: Superintendent of Banking, 418 Sixth Ave., Room 530, Des Moines, IA 50309, (515) 281-4014
Energy: Iowa Energy Policy Council, Capitol Complex, Lucas State Office Building, Des Moines, IA 50319, (515) 281-4420
Utilities: Consumer Protection Div., Attorney General's Office, Iowa Dept. of Justice, 1300 E. Walnut, Hoover Bldg., Des Moines, IA 50319, (515) 281-5926

KANSAS

Consumer Protection Div., Office of Attorney General, Kansas Judicial Center, 301 W. 10th, Topeka, KS 66612, (913) 296-3751

Johnson County Consumer Fraud Div., Johnson County Courthouse, Box 728, Olathe, KS 66061, (913) 782-5000, ext. 318
Sedgwick County Consumer Fraud and Economic Crime Div., District Attorney's Office, Sedgwick County Courthouse, Wichita, KS 67203, (316) 268-7921
Shawnee County Asst. District Attorney for Consumer Affairs, 212 Shawnee County Courthouse, Topeka, KS 66603, (913) 295-4340

Kansas City Dept. of Consumer Affairs, 701 N. 7th St., Room 969, Kansas City, KS 66101, (913) 371-2000, ext. 230
Topeka Consumer Protection Div., City Attorney's Office, 215 E. 7th St., Topeka, KS 66603, (913) 295-3883

Banking: State Bank Commissioner, 818 Kansas Ave., Suite 600, Topeka, KS 66612, (913) 296-2266

Energy: Kansas Energy Office, 503 Kansas Ave., Room 241, Topeka, KS 66603, (913) 296-2496
Utilities: Kansas State Corporation Commission, State Office Bldg., 4th floor, Topeka, KS 66612, (913) 296-3324

KENTUCKY

Consumer Protection Div., Attorney General's Office, 209 St. Clair St., Frankfort, KY 40601, (502) 564-6607 (800-372-2960)

Jefferson County   Consumer Protection Dept., 208 S. Fifth St., Room 401, Louisville, KY 40202, (502) 581-6280

Louisville   Dept. of Consumer Affairs, 701 W. Jefferson St., Louisville, KY 40202, (502) 587-3595
Owensboro   Consumer Affairs Commission, 101 E. 4th St., Owensboro, KY 42301, (502) 684-7251

Banking: Commissioner of Banking and Securities, 911 Leawood Dr., Frankfort, KY 40601, (502) 564-3390
Energy: Kentucky Dept. of Energy, Capitol Plaza Tower, 12th floor, Frankfort, KY 40601, (502) 564-7070
Utilities: Consumer Protection Div., Attorney General's Office, 209 St. Clair St., Frankfort, KY 40601, (502) 564-2196

LOUISIANA

Office of Consumer Protection, PO Box 44091, Suite 1218, Capitol Station, Baton Rouge, LA 70804, (504) 925-4401 (800-272-9868). *Branch Office:* Southern Region, 234 Loyola Ave., 7th floor, New Orleans, LA 70112, (504) 568-5575. *Branch Office:* Bureau of Marketing, PO Box 44184, Capitol Station, Baton Rouge, LA 70804, (504) 292-3600

East Baton Rouge Parish   Consumer Protection Center, 304 Old Courthouse Bldg., PO Box 1471, 215 St. Louis Ave., Baton Rouge, LA 70821, (504) 389-3451
Jefferson Parish   Consumer Protection and Commercial Fraud Div., District Attorney's Office, New Courthouse Annex, 5th floor, Gretna, LA 70053, (504) 368-1020

New Orleans Mayor's Office of Consumer Affairs, City Hall-IW12, 1300 Perdido, New Orleans, LA 70112, (504) 586-4441

Banking: Commissioner of Financial Institutions, PO Box 44095, Capitol Station, Baton Rouge, LA 70804, (504) 925-4660
Energy: Dept. of Conservation, PO Box 44275, Baton Rouge, LA 70804, (504) 342-5540
Utilities: Louisiana Public Service Commission, One American Pl., Baton Rouge, LA 70825, (504) 342-4404

MAINE

Consumer and Antitrust Div., Attorney General's Office, 505 State Office Bldg., Augusta, ME 04333, (207) 289-3716
Bureau of Consumer Protection, State House Station 35, Augusta, ME 04333, (207) 289-3731

Banking: Bureau of Banking, State House Station 36, Augusta, ME 04333, (207) 289-3811
Utilities: Maine Public Utilities Commission, State House, Augusta, ME 04333, (207) 289-3831

MARYLAND

Consumer Protection Div., Office of Attorney General, 131 E. Redwood St., Baltimore, MD 21202, (301) 383-5344. *Branch Office:* Consumer Protection Div., Attorney General's Office, 5112 Berwyn Road, College Park, MD 20740, (301) 474-3500

Anne Arundel County Board of Consumer Affairs, Arundel Center, Annapolis, MD 21401, (301) 244-7309; (301) 841-6750 in Baltimore; (202) 261-8250 in Washington, DC
Baltimore County Major Fraud Unit, 309 Court House, Baltimore, MD 21202, (301) 396-4997
Howard County Office of Consumer Affairs, Carroll Bldg., 3450 Courthouse Dr., Ellicott City, MD 21043, (301) 992-2176
Montgomery County Office of Consumer Affairs, 611 Rockville Pike, Rockville, MD 20852, (301) 279-1776

Prince George's County Consumer Protection Commission, 1142 County Administration Bldg., Upper Marlboro, MD 20870, (301) 952-4700

Banking: Bank Commissioner, 1 N. Charles St., Baltimore, MD 21201, (301) 383-2480
Energy: State Department of Natural Resources, 301 W. Preston St., Suite 1302, Baltimore, MD 21201, (301) 383-6810
Utilities: Maryland Public Service Commission, 904 State Office Bldg., 301 W. Preston St., Baltimore, MD 21201, (301) 383-2374

MASSACHUSETTS

Executive Office of Consumer Affairs, John W. McCormack Bldg., One Ashburton Pl., Room 1411, Boston, MA 02108, (617) 727-7755
Self-Help Consumer Information Office, McCormack Bldg., One Ashburton Pl., Room 1411, Boston, MA 02108, (617) 727-7780. *Branch Office:* Consumer Protection Office, 235 Chestnut St., Springfield, MA 01103, (413) 785-1951

Franklin County Consumer Protection Agency, Courthouse, Greenfield, MA 01301, (413) 774-5102
Hampden County Consumer Action Center, 721 State St., Springfield, MA 01109, (413) 737-4376
Hampshire County Consumer Protection Agency, Courthouse, Northhampton, MA 01060, (413) 584-1597

Boston Boston Consumer's Council, 182 Tremont St., Boston, MA 02111, (617) 725-3320
Fitchburg Legal Services Inc., 455 Main St., Fitchburg, MA 01420, (617) 345-1946
Lowell Community Team Work, Consumer Div., 10 Bridge St., Lowell, MA 01852, (617) 453-1791

Banking: Commissioner of Banks, 100 Cambridge St., Boston, MA 02202, (617) 727-3120
Energy: Massachusetts Office of Energy Resources, 73 Tremont St., Boston, MA 02108, (617) 727-4732
Utilities: Energy Regulatory Impact Program, Public Protection Bureau, One Ashburton Pl., Boston, MA 02108, (617) 727-1085

MICHIGAN

Consumer Protection Div., Attorney General's Office, 690 Law Bldg., Lansing, MI 48913, (517) 373-1140
Consumer's Council, 414 Hollister Bldg., 106 N. Allegan St., Lansing, MI 48933, (517) 373-0947 (800-292-5680)

Bay County Consumer Protection Unit, Bay County Bldg., Bay City, MI 48706, (517) 893-3594
Genesee County Consumer Fraud Unit, 100 Courthouse, Flint, MI 48502, (313) 766-8768
Macomb County Consumer Fraud Unit, Macomb Court Bldg., Mt. Clemens, MI 48043, (313) 469-5600
Washtenaw County Consumer Action Center, 120 Catherine St., PO Box 8645, Ann Arbor, MI 48107, (313) 994-2420
Wayne County Consumer Protection Agency, Murphy Hall of Justice, 1441 St. Antoine St., Detroit, MI 48226, (313) 224-2150

Dearborn Consumer Affairs Commission, 13615 Michigan Ave., Dearborn, MI 48126, (313) 584-1200, ext. 280
Detroit City Consumer Affairs Dept., 1600 Cadillac Tower, Detroit, MI 48226, (313) 224-3508

Banking: Financial Institutions Bureau, PO Box 30224, Lansing, MI 48909, (517) 373-3460
Energy: Energy Administration, Dept. of Commerce, 6520 Mercentile Way, Lansing, MI 48910, (517) 374-9090
Professional Services: Dept. of Licensing and Regulation, Bureau of Realty and Environmental Services, Consumer Complaint Unit, 905 Southland, PO Box 30018, Lansing, MI 48909, (517) 374-9625
Branch Office: Bureau of Commercial Services, Consumer Complaint Unit, 905 Southland, PO Box 30018, Lansing, MI 48909, (517) 374-9673
Utilities: Public Service Commission, PO Box 30221, Lansing, MI 48909, (517) 373-8729 (800-292-9555)

MINNESOTA

Office of Consumer Services, 7th & Roberts Sts., St. Paul, MN 55101, (612) 296-4512. *Branch Office:* Duluth Regional Office, 604 Alworth Bldg., Duluth, MN 55802, (218) 723-4891

Hennepin County   Citizen Protection and Economic Crime Div., C 2000 County Government Ctr., Minneapolis, MN 55487, (612) 348-8105

Minneapolis   Dept. of Licenses and Consumer Services, 101A City Hall, Minneapolis, MN 55415, (612) 348-2080

Banking: Commissioner of Banks, Metro Square Bldg., 7th & Roberts Sts., St. Paul, MN 55101, (612) 296-2715
Energy: Minnesota Energy Agency, 740 American Center Bldg., 160 E. Kellogg Blvd., St. Paul, MN 55101, (612) 296-6424
Utilities: Residential Consumer Utility Unit, Metro Square Bldg., 7th & Roberts Sts., St. Paul, MN 55101, (612) 296-4512

MISSISSIPPI

Consumer Protection Div., Office of Attorney General, Justice Bldg., PO Box 220, Jackson, MI 39205, (601) 354-7130

Banking: Dept. of Bank Supervision, PO Box 731, Jackson, MI 39205, (601) 354-6106
Energy: Fuel and Energy Management Commission, 1307 Woolfolk State Office Bldg., Jackson, MI 39205, (601) 354-7406
Utilities: Public Service Commission, Walter Sillers State Office Bldg., PO Box 1174, Jackson, MI 39205, (601) 354-7474

MISSOURI

Consumer Protection Div., Office of Attorney General, Supreme Court Bldg., PO Box 899, Jefferson City, MO 65102, (314) 751-3321. *Branch Office:* 705 Olive St., St. Louis, MO 63101, (314) 241-2211. *Branch Office:* 615 E. 13th St., Kansas City, MO 64106, (816) 274-6686
Missouri Consumer Information Center (MCIC), PO Box 1157, Jefferson City, MO 65102, (314) 751-4996. *MCIC Branch:* 615 E. 13th St., Kansas City, MO 64106, (816) 274-6381. *MCIC Branch:* 330 Mansion House Ctr., St. Louis, MO 63102, (314) 241-8318
Action Center, Consumer Affairs Dept., 414 E. 12th St., Kansas City, MO 64106, (816) 274-2222

Banking: Commissioner of Finance, PO Box 716, Jefferson City, MO 65101, (314) 751-3397

Energy: Missouri Energy Program, PO Box 176, Jefferson City, MO 65101, (314) 751-4000

Utilities: Missouri Public Service Commission, Jefferson Bldg., PO Box 360, Jefferson City, MO 65101, (314) 751-3234

MONTANA

Consumer Affairs Div., Dept. of Business Regulation, 805 N. Main St., Helena, MT 59601, (406) 449-3163

Energy: Energy Div., 32 S. Ewing, Helena, MT 50601, (406) 449-3780

Utilities: Montana Consumer Counsel, 34 W. 6th Ave., Helena, MT 59601, (406) 449-2771

NEBRASKA

Consumer Protection Div., State House, Lincoln, NB 68509, (402) 471-2682

Consumer Protection Div., Dept. of Justice, 605 S. 14th, Lincoln, NB 68509, (402) 471-2682

Douglas County Consumer Fraud Div., County Attorney's Office, 909 Omaha-Douglas Civic Center, Omaha, NB 68183, (402) 444-7625

Banking: Banking and Finance, PO Box 95006, Lincoln, NB 68509, (402) 471-2171

Energy: Nebraska Energy Office, PO Box 95085, Lincoln, NB 68509, (402) 471-2867

Utilities: Nebraska Public Service Commission, PO Box 94927, Lincoln, NB 65809, (402) 471-3101

NEVADA

Consumer-Affairs Div., Attorney General's Office, 2501 E. Sahara Ave., Las Vegas, NV 89158, (702) 386-5293

Consumer Affairs Div., Dept. of Commerce, 2501 E. Sahara Ave., Las Vegas, NV 89158, (702) 386-5293. *Branch Office:* 201 Nye Bldg., Capitol Complex, Carson City, NV 89710, (702) 885-4340 (800-992-0973)

Washoe County   Consumer Protection Div., District Attorney's Office, PO Box 11130, Reno, NV 89520, (702) 785-5652

Banking: Superintendent of Banks, Capitol Complex, Carson City, NV 89710, (702) 885-4260
Energy: Nevada Dept. of Energy, 1050 E. Willard, Suite 405, Carson City, NV 89710, (702) 885-5157
Utilities: Div. of Consumer Relations, Public Service Commission, 505 E. King St., Carson City, NV 89710, (702) 885-5556

NEW HAMPSHIRE

Consumer Protection, Office of Attorney General, State House Annex, Concord, NH 03301, (603) 271-3641

Banking: Bank Commissioner, 97 N. Main St., Concord, NH 03301, (603) 271-3561
Energy: Governor's Council on Energy, 2½ Beacon St., Concord, NH 03301, (603) 271-2711
Utilities: Legislative Utility Consumers Council, 109 N. Main St., Concord, NH 03301, (603) 271-2762

NEW JERSEY

Div. of Consumer Affairs, Dept. of Law and Public Safety, 1100 Raymond Blvd., Newark, NJ 07102, (201) 648-4010
Dept. of Public Advocate, PO Box 141, Trenton, NJ 08625, (609) 292-7087 (800-792-8600)
Div. of Consumer Complaints, Legal and Economic Research, PO Box CN040, Trenton, NJ 08625, (609) 292-5341

Atlantic County   Office of Consumer Affairs, 1601 Atlantic Ave., Atlantic City, NJ 08401, (609) 345-6700, ext. 475
Bergen County   Office of Consumer Affairs, 355 Main St., Hackensack, NJ 07601, (201) 646-2650
Burlington County   Office of Consumer Affairs, 54 Grant St., Mt. Holly, NJ 08060, (609) 267-3300, ext. 259
Camden County   Office of Consumer Affairs, 600 Market St., Camden County Administration Bldg., Camden, NJ 08101, (609) 757-8387

Cumberland County Dept. of Weights and Measures and Consumer Protection, 788 E. Commerce St., Bridgeton, NJ 08302, (609) 451-8000, ext. 369

Hudson County Office of Consumer Affairs, County Courthouse, 595 Newark Ave., Jersey City, NJ 07306, (201) 792-3737

Hunterdon County Office of Consumer Affairs, Skyview, R.D., Lebanon, NJ 08833, (201) 735-4478

Mercer County Div. of Consumer Affairs, 640 S. Broad St., Trenton, NJ 08607, (609) 989-6671

Middlesex County Office of Consumer Affairs, 841 Georges Rd., N. Brunswick, NJ 08902, (201) 745-2787

Monmouth County Office of Consumer Affairs, Hall of Records, Main St., Freehold, NJ 07728, (201) 431-7900

Morris County Office of Consumer Affairs, Administration Bldg., Ann St., Morristown, NJ 07960, (201) 285-2811

Ocean County Dept. of Consumer Affairs, C.N. 2191, Toms River, NJ 08753, (201) 929-2105

Passaic County Consumer Affairs Div., Administration Bldg., 309 Pennsylvania Ave., Paterson, NJ 07503, (201) 525-5000

Somerset County Dept. of Consumer Affairs, County Administration Bldg., Somerville, NJ 08876, (201) 725-4700, ext. 306

Union County Div. of Consumer Affairs, 300 N. Avenue E, Westfield, NJ 07091, (201) 233-0502

Fort Lee Consumer Protection Board, 309 Main St., Ft. Lee, NJ 07024, (201) 592-3540

Paterson Dept. of Human Resources, Consumer Affairs, 1 W. Broadway, Paterson, NJ 07505, (201) 881-3700

Banking: Commissioner of Banking, 36 W. State St., Trenton, NJ 08625, (609) 292-3420

Energy: Dept. of Energy, 101 Commerce St., Newark, NJ 07102, (201) 648-2744

Utilities: Consumer Services, Public Utilities Commission, 1100 Raymond Blvd., Newark, NJ 07102, (201) 648-2096

NEW MEXICO

Consumer and Economic Crime Div., PO Box 1508, Santa Fe, NM 87501, (505) 827-5521

Bernalillo County   Public Services Div., District Attorney's Office, 415 Tijeras, Albuquerque, NM 87102, (505) 766-4326
Valencia County   District Attorney for Consumer Protection, PO Box 718, Los Lunas, NM 87031, (505) 865-9643

Banking: Financial Institutions Div., Commerce and Industry Dept., Lew Wallace Bldg., Santa Fe, NM 87503, (505) 827-2217
Energy: Dept. of Energy and Minerals, PO Box 2770, Santa Fe, NM 87501, (505) 827-2471
Utilities: Director of Energy Unit, PO Drawer 1508, Santa Fe, NM 87501, (505) 827-5521

NEW YORK

Consumer Protection Board, 99 Washington Ave., Albany, NY 12210, (518) 474-8583. *Branch Office:* Two World Trade Center, Room 8225, New York, NY 10047, (212) 488-5666
Consumer Frauds and Protection Bureau, Office of Attorney General, State Capitol, Albany, NY 12224, (518) 474-8686
Branch Offices (write Assistant Attorney General in charge of Consumer Frauds and Protection at appropriate address):
    10 Lower Metcalf Pl., Auburn, NY 13021, (315) 253-9765
    44 Hawley St., Binghamton, NY 13901, (607) 773-7823
    65 Court St., Buffalo, NY 14202, (716) 842-4396
    Suffolk State Office Bldg., Hauppauge, NY 11787, (516) 979-5190
    48 Cornelia St., Plattsburgh, NY 12901, (518) 561-1980
    65 Broad St., Rochester, NY 14614, (716) 454-4540
    333 E. Washington St., Syracuse, NY 13202, (315) 473-8181
    40 Garden St., Poughkeepsie, NY 12601, (914) 452-7744
    207 Genesee St., Box 528, Utica, NY 13501, (315) 797-6120
    317 Washington St., Watertown, NY 13601, (315) 782-0100

Erie County   Consumer Fraud Bureau, 25 Delaware Ave., Buffalo, NY 14202, (716) 855-2424
    Consumer Protection Committee, 95 Franklin St., Buffalo, NY 14202, (716) 846-6690
Kings County   Consumer Frauds and Economic Crimes Bureau, 210 Joralemon St., Brooklyn, NY 11201, (212) 834-5000
Nassau County   Office of Consumer Affairs, 160 Old Country Rd., Mineola, NY 11501, (516) 535-3100

Commercial Frauds Bureau, 1425 Old Country Rd., Plainview, NY 11803, (516) 420-5058

Oneida County   County Office Bldg., 800 Park Ave., Utica, NY 13501, (315) 798-5601

Onondaga County   Office of Consumer Affairs, County Civic Center, 421 Montgomery St., Syracuse, NY 13202, (315) 425-3479

Orange County   District Attorney's Office of Consumer Affairs, County Government Center, Goshen, NY 10924, (914) 294-5471

Putnam County   Dept. of Consumer Affairs, 206 County Office Bldg., Carmel, NY 10512, (914) 225-3641, ext. 215

Rensselaer County   Citizens Affairs, 1600 7th Ave., Troy, NY 12180, (518) 270-5444

Rockland County   Office of Consumer Protection, County Office Bldg., 18 New Hempstead Rd., New City, NY 10956, (914) 425-5280

Steuben County   Dept. of Weights and Measures and Consumer Affairs, 19 E. Morris St., Bath, NY 14810, (607) 776-4949

Suffolk County   Dept. of Consumer Affairs, Suffolk County Ctr., Hauppauge, NY 11787, (516) 979-3100

Ulster County   Consumer Fraud Bureau, 285 Wall St., Kingston, NY 12401, (914) 331-2926

Warren County   Director of Weights and Measures and Consumer Protection, Municipal Center, Lake George, NY 12845, (518) 792-9951

Westchester County   Office of Consumer Affairs, County Office Bldg., White Plains, NY 10601, (914) 682-3300

Babylon   Consumer Protection Board, 200 E. Sunrise Hwy., Lindenhurst, NY 11757, (516) 957-3021

Colonie   Consumer Protection Agency, Memorial Town Hall, Newtonville, NY 12128, (518) 783-2790

Croton-on-Hudson   Consumer Affairs Bureau, Municipal Bldg., Croton-on-Hudson, NY 10520, (914) 739-7900

Greenburg   Consumer Board, PO Box 205, Elmsford, NY 10523, (914) 693-7808

Huntington   Consumer Protection Board, 423 Park Ave., Huntington, NY 11743, (516) 421-1000, ext. 271

Mt. Vernon   Office of Consumer Affairs, City Hall, Mt. Vernon, NY 10550, (914) 668-2200, ext. 201

New Rochelle   104 County Office Bldg., White Plains, NY 10601, (914) 682-3300

New York City   Dept. of Consumer Affairs, 80 Lafayette St., New York, NY 10013, (212) 566-5456
   Branch Offices: Brooklyn Complaint Center, 185 Montague St., Brooklyn, NY 11201, (212) 596-4780
   120-55 Queens Blvd., Kew Gardens, NY 11424, (212) 261-2922
   1932 Arthur Ave., Bronx, NY 10457, (212) 299-1400
   227 E. 116th St., New York, NY 10029, (212) 348-0600
   Staten Island Bureau Hall, Staten Island, NY 10301, (212) 390-5154
Orangeburg   Consumer Protection Board, Orangeburg Town Hall, 26 Orangeburg Rd., Orangeburg, NY 10962, (914) 359-5100
Oswego   Office of Consumer Affairs, 104 City Hall, Lake St., Oswego, NY 13126, (315) 342-2410
Ramapo   Consumer Protection Board, Ramapo Town Hall, Suffern, NY 10901, (914) 357-5100, ext. 267
Schenectady   Bureau of Consumer Protection, 22 City Hall, Jay St., Schenectady, NY 12305, (518) 382-5061
Syracuse   Consumer Affairs Office, 422 City Hall, 223 E. Washington St., Syracuse, NY 13202, (315) 473-3240
Yonkers   Office of Consumer Protection, 201 Palisade Ave., Yonkers, NY 10703, (914) 965-0707

Banking: Superintendent of Banks, Two World Trade Center, New York, NY 10047, (212) 488-2310
Energy: Energy Office, Agency Bldg., No. 2, Empire State Plaza, Albany, NY 12223, (518) 474-8813
Utilities (outside New York City): Public Service Commission, Empire State Pl., Albany, NY 12223 (800-522-8707)
Utilities (in New York City): (212) 488-4332 for electrical; (212) 488-4392 for natural gas; (212) 488-5330 for telephone

NORTH CAROLINA

Consumer Protection Div., Office of Attorney General, Justice Bldg., PO Box 629, Raleigh, NC 27602, (919) 733-7741

Banking: Commissioner of Banks, PO Box 951, Raleigh, NC 27602, (919) 733-3016
Energy: Energy Management Div., Dept. of Commerce, 430 N. Salisbury St., Raleigh, NC 27601, (919) 733-2230
Utilities: Consumer Services, Public Utilities Commission Staff, PO Box 991, Raleigh, NC 27602, (919) 733-4271

NORTH DAKOTA

Consumer Fraud Div., Attorney General's Office, State Capitol Bldg., Bismarck, ND 58505, (701) 224-3404 (800-472-2600)
Consumer Affairs Office, State Laboratories Dept., Box 937, Bismarck, ND 58505, (701) 224-2485 (800-472-2927)

Quad County Community Action Agency, 27½ S. 3rd, Grand Forks, ND 58201, (701) 746-5431

Banking: Commissioner of Banking and Financial Institutions, State Capitol Bldg., Bismarck, ND 58505, (701) 224-2253
Energy: State Office of Energy Management, 1533 N. 12th St., Bismarck, ND 58501, (701) 224-2250
Utilities: Public Service Commission, State Capitol Bldg., Bismarck, ND 58505, (701) 224-2400

OHIO

Consumer Frauds and Crimes Section, Attorney General's Office, 30 E. Broad St., Columbus, OH 43215, (614) 466-8831

Franklin County Economic Crime Div., Prosecutor's Office, Hall of Justice, 369 S. High St., Columbus, OH 43215, (614) 462-3248
Greene County Consumer Protection and Education Office, 194 E. Church St., Xenia, OH 45385, (513) 376-1351
Lake County Consumer Protection Div., Lake County Courthouse, Painesville, OH 44077, (216) 352-6281, ext. 281
Mahoning County Consumer Fraud Div., County Courthouse, 120 Market St., Youngstown, OH 44503, (216) 747-2000, ext. 431
Medina County Prosecutor's Office, 215 Washington St., Medina, OH 44256, (216) 723-3641
Montgomery County Fraud Section, County Courts Bldg., 41 N. Perry, Dayton, OH 45422, (513) 228-5126
Portage County Consumer Protection Div., 247 S. Chestnut St., Ravenna, OH 44266, (216) 296-4593
Summit County Bureau of Investigations, 53 E. Center St., Akron, OH 44308, (216) 379-5230

Akron Div. of Weights and Measures and Consumer Protection, 1420 Triplett Blvd., Akron, OH 44306, (216) 375-2878

Canton City Sealer and Commissioner of Consumer Protection, 919 Walnut Ave. NE, Canton, OH 44704, (216) 489-3065
Cincinnati Consumer Protection Div., City Solicitor's Office, 236 City Hall, Cincinnati, OH 45202, (513) 352-3971
Cleveland Office of Consumer Affairs, 119 City Hall, 601 Lakeside Ave., Cleveland, OH 44114, (216) 664-3200
Columbus Community Services, 50 W. Gay St., Columbus, OH 43215, (614) 222-8350
Dayton Div. of Consumer Services, 7 E. 4th St., Dayton, OH 45402, (513) 225-5048
Toledo Consumer Protection Agency, 151 N. Michigan Ave., Toledo, OH 43624, (419) 247-6191
Youngstown Div. of Consumer Affairs, 496 Glenwood Ave., Youngstown, OH 44502, (216) 747-3561

Banking: Superintendent of Banks, 180 E. Broad St., Columbus, OH 43215, (614) 466-2932
Energy: Dept. of Energy, State Office Tower, 30 E. Broad St., Columbus, OH 43215, (614) 466-1805
Utilities: Public Utilities Commission, 180 E. Broad St., Columbus, OH 43215, (614) 466-3016

OKLAHOMA

Dept. of Consumer Affairs, 460 Jim Thorpe Bldg., Oklahoma City, OK 73105, (405) 521-3653

Banking: Commissioner of Banking, 4100 N. Lincoln Blvd., Oklahoma City, OK 73105, (405) 521-2782
Energy: Dept. of Energy, 4400 N. Lincoln Blvd., Suite 251, Oklahoma City, OK 73105, (405) 521-3941

OREGON

Consumer Protection Div., Attorney General's Office, 520 SW Yamhill St., Portland, OR 97204, (503) 229-5522
Consumer Services Div., Dept. of Commerce, Labor and Industries Bldg., Salem, OR 97310, (503) 378-4320

*Banking:*Superintendent of Banks, Dept. of Commerce, Busick Bldg., Salem, OR 97310, (503) 378-4140
Energy: Dept. of Energy, Labor and Industries Bldg., Salem, OR 97310, (503) 378-4131
Utilities: Public Utility Commission, 300 Labor and Industries Bldg., Salem, OR 97310, (503) 378-6611

PENNSYLVANIA

Bureau of Consumer Protection, 301 Market St., Harrisburg, PA 17101, (717) 787-9707.
Branch Offices (write Assistant Attorney General, Bureau of Consumer Protection, Dept. of Justice at appropriate address):
133 N. 5th St., Allentown, PA 18102, (215) 821-0901
919 State St., Erie, PA 16501, (814) 871-4371
Strawberry Square, 15th floor, Harrisburg, PA 17121, (717) 787-7109
1405 Locust St., Philadelphia, PA 19102, (215) 238-6475
300 Liberty Ave., Pittsburgh, PA 15222, (412) 565-5135
100 Lackawanna Ave., 105A State Office Bldg., Scranton, PA 18503, (717) 961-4913
Commerce Bldg., 919 State St., Erie, PA 16501, (814) 871-4371
615 Howard Ave., Altoona, PA 16601, (814) 943-1133

Allegheny County Bureau of Consumer Affairs, 320 Jones Law Annex, 311 Ross St., Pittsburgh, PA 15219, (412) 355-5402
Armstrong County Community Action Agency, 125 Queen St., Kittanning, PA 16201, (412) 548-8696
Berks County Consumer Action, City Hall, 8th & Washington, Reading, PA 19601, (215) 373-5111, ext. 369
Bucks County Dept. of Consumer Protection, Broad & Union Sts., Doylestown, PA 18901, (215) 348-2911
Carbon County Consumer Referral Service, 61 Broadway, Jim Thorpe, PA 18229, (717) 325-3678
Cumberland County Bureau of Consumer Affairs, 35 E. High St., Carlisle, PA 17013, (717) 249-1133
Delaware County Office of Consumer Affairs, 2nd & Orange Sts., Media, PA 19063, (215) 891-2430
Lancaster County Consumer Protection Commission, County Courthouse, Lancaster PA 17602, (717) 299-7921

Montgomery County Consumer Affairs Dept., County Courthouse, Norristown, PA 19404, (215) 278-3565
Schuykill County Consumer Protection Agency, County Courthouse, Pottsville, PA 17901, (717) 462-1952
Westmoreland County Bureau of Consumer Affairs, 102 W. Otterman St., PO Box Q, Greensburg, PA 15601, (412) 836-6170
York County Consumer Protection Office, Courthouse, 28 E. Market St., York, PA 17401, (717) 848-3301

Philadelphia Mayor's Office of Consumer Services, 143 City Hall, Philadelphia, PA 19107, (215) 686-2798

Banking: Consumer Affairs, Dept. of Banking, PO Box 2155, Harrisburg, PA 17120, (717) 787-1854
Energy: Governor's Energy Council, 1625 N. Front, Harrisburg, PA 17120, (717) 783-8610
Utilities: Bureau of Consumer Services, Public Utility Commission, North Office Bldg., Harrisburg, PA 17120, (717) 783-5391

RHODE ISLAND

Public Protection Consumer Unit, Dept. of Attorney General, 56 Pine St., Providence, RI 02903, (401) 277-3163

Banking: Bank Commissioner, 100 N. Main St., Providence, RI 02903, (401) 277-2405
Energy: State Energy Office, Providence, RI 02903, (401) 277-3374
Utilities: Consumer Affairs, Div. of Public Utilities, 100 Orange St., Providence, RI 02903, (401) 277-2443

SOUTH CAROLINA

Office of Citizen's Service, Governor's Office, PO Box 11450, Columbia, SC 29211, (803) 758-3261
Dept. of Consumer Affairs, 2221 Devine St., Columbia, SC 29211, (803) 758-2040 (800-922-1594)
State Ombudsman, Office of Executive Policy and Programs, 1205 Pendleton St., Columbia, SC 29201, (803) 758-2249

Banking: Commissioner of Banking, 1026 Sumter St., Columbia, SC 29201, (803) 758-2186

Energy: Div. of Energy Resources, SCN Center, 1122 Lady St., Columbia, SC 29201, (803) 758-7502

SOUTH DAKOTA

Div. of Consumer Protection, Capitol Bldg., Pierre, SD 57501, (605) 773-3215. *Branch Office:* 114 S. Main Ave., Sioux Falls, SD 57102, (605) 339-6691

Banking: Banking and Finance, State Capitol Bldg., Pierre, SD 57501, (605) 773-3421

Energy: Office of Energy Policy, State Capitol, Pierre, SD 57501, (605) 773-3603

Utilities: Assistant Attorney General, Public Utilities Commission, State Capitol, Pierre, SD 57501, (605) 773-3201

TENNESSEE

Div. of Consumer Affairs, Dept. of Agriculture, Box 40627, Melrose Station, Nashville, TN 37204, (615) 741-1461 (800-342-8385)

Nashville   Mayor's Office of Consumer Affairs, 107 Metro Courthouse, Nashville, TN 37201, (615) 259-6047

Banking: Commissioner of Banking, 460 Capitol Hill Bldg., 311 7th Ave., Nashville, TN 37219, (615) 741-2236

Energy: Energy Authority, 707 Capitol Blvd. Bldg., Nashville, TN 37219, (615) 741-1772

Utilities: Public Service Commission, C1-100 Cordell Hull Bldg., Nashville, TN 37219, (615) 741-2785

TEXAS

Consumer Protection and Antitrust Div., Attorney General's Office, PO Box 12548 Capitol Station, Austin, TX 78711, (512) 475-3288
Branch Offices (write Assistant Attorney General, Consumer Protection Div. at appropriate address):
4313 N. 10th, Suite F, McAllen, TX 78501, (512) 682-4547

701 Commerce, Suite 200, Dallas, TX 75202, (214) 742-8944
4824 Alberta Ave., El Paso, TX 79905, (915) 533-3484
312 County Office Bldg., 806 Broadway, Lubbock, TX 79401,
(806) 747-5238
200 Main Plaza, Suite 400, San Antonio, TX 78205, (512) 225-4191
723 Main St., Suite 610, Houston, TX 77002, (713) 228-0701
201 E. Belknap St., Ft. Worth, TX 76102, (817) 334-1788

Bexar County Consumer Fraud Div., Office of Criminal District
Attorney, San Antonio, TX 78205, (512) 220-2323
Dallas County Consumer Fraud Div., 2700 Stemmons Expswy.,
500 Stemmons Tower E., Dallas, TX 75207, (214) 630-6300
El Paso, Culberson, and Hudspeth Counties Consumer Protection
Div., El Paso County Annex Bldg., 4824 Alberta St., El Paso, TX
79905, (915) 533-3484
Harris County Consumer Fraud Div., 201 Fannin Bank Bldg.,
Houston, TX 77002, (713) 221-5836
Tarrant County Economic Crimes, 200 W. Belknap St., Ft. Worth,
TX 76102, (817) 334-1261
Travis County Consumer Affairs Office, 624B N. Pleasant Valley
Rd., Austin, TX 78702, (512) 474-6554
Waller, Austin, and Fayette Counties County Courthouse, Box 171,
District Attorney's Office, Hempstead, TX 77445, (713) 826-3335

Dallas Dept. of Consumer Affairs, City Hall, Room 2BN, Dallas,
TX 75201, (214) 670-4433
Fort Worth Office of Consumer Affairs, 1800 University Dr.,
Room 208, Ft. Worth, TX 76107, (817) 870-7570

Banking: Banking Commissioner, 2601 N. Lamar, Austin, TX
78705, (512) 475-4451
Energy: Texas Energy Advisory Council, 7703 N. Lamar Blvd.,
Austin, TX 78752, (512) 475-7017
*Utilities:*Public Utility Commission, 7800 Shoal Creek Blvd., Suite
400 N, Austin, TX 78757, (512) 458-6111

UTAH

Div. of Consumer Affairs, Dept. of Business Regulation, 330 E. Fourth St., Salt Lake City, UT 84111, (801) 533-6441
Consumer Protection Unit, Office of Attorney General, 236 State Capitol, Salt Lake City, UT 84114, (801) 533-5261

Banking: Commissioner of Financial Institutions, 10 W. Broadway, Suite 331, Salt Lake City, UT 84101, (801) 533-5461
Energy: Utah Energy Office, 231 W. 400 South, Room 101, Salt Lake City, UT 84111, (801) 533-5424
Utilities: Utah Committee of Consumer Services, 330 E. 4th St., Salt Lake City, UT 84111, (801) 533-5511

VERMONT

Consumer Protection Div., Office of Attorney General, 109 State St., Montpelier, VT 05602, (802) 828-3171 (800-642-5149)

Banking: Commissioner of Banking and Insurance, 120 State St., State Office Bldg., Montpelier, VT 05602, (802) 828-3301
Energy: State Energy Office, State Office Bldg., Montpelier, VT 05602, (802) 828-2393
Utilities: Consumer Affairs Div., Vermont Public Service Board, 120 State St., Montpelier, VT 05602, (802) 828-2332

VIRGINIA

Consumer Counsel, 11 S. 12th St., Suite 308, Richmond, VA 23219, (804) 786-4075
State Office of Consumer Affairs, Dept. of Agriculture and Consumer Services, 825 E. Broad St., Box 1163, Richmond, VA 23209, (804) 786-2042 (800-552-9963)

Arlington County Office of Consumer Affairs, 2049 15th St. N., Arlington VA 22201, (703) 558-2142
Fairfax County Dept. of Consumer Affairs, 4031 University Dr., Fairfax, VA 22030, (703) 691-3214
Prince William County Office of Consumer Affairs, 15960 Cardinal Dr., Woodbridge, VA 22191, (703) 221-4156

Alexandria Office of Consumer Affairs, PO Box 178, City Hall, Alexandria, VA 22313, (703) 750-6675

Newport News Office of Consumer Affairs, City Hall, 2400 Washington Ave., Newport News, VA 23607, (804) 247-8616

Norfolk Div. of Consumer Affairs, 804 City Hall Bldg., Norfolk, VA 23501, (804) 441-2823

Roanoke Consumer Protection Div., 353 Municipal Bldg., 215 Church Ave. SW, Roanoke, VA 24011, (703) 981-2583

Virginia Beach Div. of Consumer Protection, City Hall, Virginia Beach, VA 23456, (804) 427-4421

Banking: Commissioner of Financial Institutions, Suite 1600, 701 E. Byrd St., Richmond, VA 23219, (804) 786-3657

Energy: Office of Emergency and Energy Services, 310 Turner Rd., Richmond, VA 23225, (804) 745-3305

Utilities: Assistant Attorney General, Div. of Consumer Counsel, 11 S. 12th St., Suite 308, Richmond, VA 23219, (804) 786-4075

WASHINGTON

Consumer Protection and Antitrust Div., Office of Attorney General, 1366 Dexter Horton Bldg., Seattle, WA 98104, (206) 464-7744 (800-552-0700)

Branch Offices (write Consumer Office of Attorney General at appropriate address):

Temple of Justice, Olympia, WA 98504, (206) 753-6210

960 Paulsen Professional Bldg., Spokane, WA 99201, (509) 456-3123

620 Perkins Bldg., Tacoma, WA 98402, (206) 593-2904

215 Union Avenue Bldg., Olympia, WA 98504, (206) 753-0929

King County Fraud Div., Prosecuting Attorney's Office, E 531 King County Courthouse, Seattle, WA 98104, (206) 583-4513

Everett Weights and Measures Dept., City Hall, 3002 Wetmore Ave., Everett, WA 98201, (206) 259-8845

Seattle Dept. of Licenses and Consumer Affairs, 102 Municipal Bldg., Seattle, WA 98104, (206) 625-2536; (206) 625-2712, complaint line

Banking: Supervisor of Banking, 219 General Administration Bldg., Olympia, WA 98504, (206) 753-6520

Energy: Energy Office, 400 E. Union St., Olympia, WA 98504, (206) 753-2417

Utilities: Utilities and Transportation Commission, Highways-Licenses Bldg., Mail Stop PB 02, Olympia, WA 98504, (206) 753-6423

WEST VIRGINIA

Consumer Protection Div., Office of Attorney General, 3412 Staunton Ave. SE, Charleston, WV 25305, (304) 348-8986

Consumer Protection Div., Dept. of Labor, 1900 Washington St. E., Charleston, WV 25305, (304) 348-7890

Charleston   Consumer Protection Dept., PO Box 2749, Charleston, WV 25330, (304) 348-8173

Banking: Commissioner of Banking, State Office Bldg. 6, 1900 Washington St. E., Charleston, WV 25305, (304) 348-2294

Energy: Fuel and Energy Div., Governor's Office of Economic and Community Development, 1262½ Greenbriar St., Charleston, WV 25305, (304) 348-8860

Utilities: Public Service Commission, E-217 State Capitol Bldg., Charleston, WV 25305, (304) 348-2182

WISCONSIN

Office of Consumer Protection, Dept. of Justice, State Capitol, Madison, WI 53702, (608) 266-1852. *Branch Office:* Milwaukee State Office Bldg., 819 N. 6th St., Milwaukee, WI 53203, (414) 224-1867

Div. of Consumer Protection, Dept. of Agriculture, PO Box 8911, Madison, WI 53708, (608) 266-9837 (800-362-8025). *Branch Offices* (write Division of Consumer Protection at appropriate address):

1727 Loring St., Altoona, WI 54720, (715) 836-2861

1181A Western Ave., Green Bay, WI 54303, (414) 497-4210

10320 W. Silver Spring Drive, Milwaukee, WI 53225, (414) 257-8966

Kenosha County Consumer Investigator, 912 56th St., Kenosha, WI 53140, (414) 656-6480

Marathon County District Attorney's Office, County Court House, Wausau, WI 54401, (715) 842-0471

Milwaukee County Consumer Fraud Unit, 821 W. State St., Room 412, Milwaukee, WI 53233, (414) 278-4792

Portage County Consumer Fraud Unit, County Court House, Stevens Point, WI 54481, (715) 346-3393

Racine County Consumer Fraud Div., 730 Wisconsin Ave., Racine, WI 53403, (414) 636-3125

Banking: Commissioner of Banking, 30 W. Mifflin St., Room 401, Madison, WI 53703, (608) 266-1621

Energy: Div. of State Executive Budget and Planning, Madison, WI 53702, (608) 266-3382

Utilities: Public Service Commission, 432 Hill Farms State Office Bldg., Madison, WI 53702, (608) 266-1241

WYOMING

Assistant Attorney General, 123 Capitol Bldg., Cheyenne, WY 82002, (307) 777-7841

Banking: State Examiner, 819 W. Pershing Ave., Cheyenne, WY 82002, (307) 777-7797

Energy: State Planning Coordinator, 2320 Capitol Ave., Cheyenne, WY 82002, (307) 777-7574

Utilities: Public Service Commission, Capitol Hill Bldg., 320 W. 25th St., Cheyenne, WY 82002, (307) 777-7427

Federal Information Centers

Federal Information Centers (FICs) provide a network of consumer-information and consumer-referral services in eighty-five cities across the country. The centers may be able to provide specific information on a specific problem, but their prime value is in providing the name, address, and phone number of a consumer agency (whether federal, state, or local) that is best equipped to help you. The following numbers are local, toll-free lines. Some are FIC numbers; others (still toll-free) are tie-lines to the nearest FIC.

Akron	216-375-5638	Hartford	203-527-2617
Albany	518-463-4421	Honolulu	808-546-8620
Albuquerque	505-766-3091	Houston	713-226-5711
Allentown	215-821-7785	Indianapolis	317-269-7373
Atlanta	404-221-6891	Jacksonville	904-354-4756
Austin	512-472-5494	Kansas City	816-374-2466
Baltimore	301-962-4980	Little Rock	501-378-6177
Birmingham	205-322-8591	Los Angeles	213-688-3800
Boston	617-223-7121	Louisville	502-582-6261
Buffalo	716-846-4010	Memphis	901-521-3285
Charlotte	704-376-3600	Miami	305-350-4155
Chattanooga	615-265-8231	Milwaukee	414-271-2273
Chicago	312-353-4242	Minneapolis	612-725-2073
Cincinnati	513-684-2801	Mobile	205-438-1421
Cleveland	216-522-4040	Nashville	615-242-5056
Colorado Springs	303-471-9491	Newark	201-645-3600
Columbus	614-221-1014	New Haven	203-624-4720
Dallas	214-767-8585	New Orleans	504-589-6696
Dayton	513-223-7377	Newport News	804-244-0480
Denver	303-837-3602	New York	212-264-4464
Des Moines	515-284-4448	Norfolk	804-441-3101
Detroit	313-226-7016	Ogden	801-399-1347
Ft. Lauderdale	305-522-8531	Oklahoma City	405-231-4868
Ft. Worth	817-334-3624	Omaha	402-221-3353
Gary	219-883-4110	Orlando	305-442-1800
Grand Rapids	616-451-2628	Paterson	201-523-0717

Philadelphia	215-597-7042	San Jose	408-275-7422
Phoenix	602-261-3313	Santa Ana	714-836-2386
Pittsburgh	412-644-3456	Santa Fe	505-983-7743
Portland	503-221-2222	Scranton	717-346-7081
Providence	401-331-5565	Seattle	206-442-0570
Pueblo	303-544-9523	Syracuse	315-476-8545
Richmond	804-643-4928	Tacoma	206-383-5230
Roanoke	703-982-8591	Tampa	813-229-7911
Rochester	716-546-5075	Toledo	419-241-3223
Sacramento	916-440-3344	Topeka	913-295-2866
St. Joseph	816-233-8206	Trenton	609-396-4400
St. Louis	314-425-4106	Tucson	602-622-1511
St. Petersburg	813-893-3495	Tulsa	918-584-4193
Salt Lake City	801-524-5353	Washington	202-755-8660
San Antonio	512-224-4471	West Palm Beach	305-833-7566
San Diego	714-293-6030	Wichita	316-263-6931
San Francisco	415-556-6600		

Index

About the Author

MIKE MCCLINTOCK is currently the host of "The Home Show" on WMCA Radio in New York and has had extensive experience as a general building contractor. He is the author of *The Homeowner's Handbook* and has written more than two hundred articles on home care and repair for *Playboy, Family Handyman, Popular Mechanics,* and other publications. Mike has also been the "Home and Shop" editor for *Popular Mechanics* and will shortly be seen on the Warner-Amex Cable Network as their editor for home care and repair.